PILOT'S FLIGHT OPERATING INSTRUCTIONS

FOR
ARMY MODEL
B-29
AIRPLANES

JANUARY 25, 1944

This publication shall not be carried in aircraft on combat missions or when there is a reasonable chance of its falling into the hands of the enemy.

NOTE: This Handbook replaces AN 01-20EJ-1 dated August 20, 1943.

NOTICE: This document contains information affecting the national defense of the United States within the meaning of the Espionage Act, 50 U. S. C., 31 and 32, as amended. Its transmission or the revelation of its contents in any manner to an unauthorized person is prohibited by law.

Published under joint authority of the Commanding General, Army Air Forces, the Chief of the Bureau of Aeronautics, and the Air Council of the United Kingdom.

THIS PUBLICATION MAY BE USED BY PERSONNEL RENDERING SERVICE TO THE UNITED STATES OR ITS ALLIES

LIST OF REVISED PAGES ISSUED

NOTE: A heavy black vertical line, to the left of the text on revised pages, indicates the extent of the revision. This line is omitted where more than 50 percent of the page is revised.

TABLE OF CONTENTS

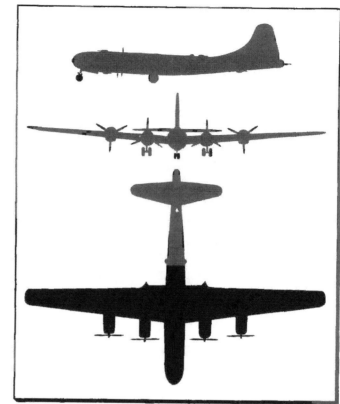

Figure 1—B-29 Bombardment Airplane

SECTION I

DESCRIPTION

1. AIRPLANE.

a. GENERAL.—The B-29 heavy bombardment airplane is a midwing monoplane with a design useful weight of 105,000 pounds and a maximum alternate gross weight of 128,000 pounds fully loaded. Power is supplied by four R-3350-23 Wright engines. (YB-29 airplanes are powered by R-3350-21 engines.) Pressurized compartments permit extreme altitudes with little discomfort to the crew. The landing gear is of the tricycle type and is fully retractable.

(1) Provisions are made for a normal crew of 6 or an alternate crew of 12. The normal crew consists of a pilot, copilot, engineer, navigator, radio operator, and bombardier.

(2) The airplane is equipped with five, power-operated gun turrets, remotely controlled, with each turret housing two .50-caliber machine guns. The tail turret also houses one 20-mm cannon. Five sighting stations are provided: three in the rear pressurized compartment, one in the tail compartment, and one at the bombardier's station.

(3) The airplane is capable of carrying the following bomb loads:

80	100-pound bombs
56	300-pound bombs
40	500-pound bombs
12	1000-pound bombs
12	1600-pound bombs
8	2000-pound bombs
4	4000-pound bombs

b. WING.—The wing consists of an inboard section permanently attached to the fuselage and two removable outer panels provided with detachable tips. Fuel compartments equipped with self-sealing tanks are an integral part of the inboard wing section structure. Ailerons provided with trim tabs, are hinged to the outboard panels, and electrically operated wing flaps form the lower surface of the inboard wing trailing edge from the fuselage to the outboard wing joint. The leading edge sections are removable and provide access to cables, wiring, tubing, and miscellaneous equipment.

c. EMPENNAGE.—The empennage is the conventional type which includes a horizontal stabilizer, elevators, elevator trim tabs, a vertical stabilizer, dorsal fin, rudder, and rudder trim tab.

d. FUSELAGE.—The fuselage is of all-metal, semimonocoque design, with stressed skin, extruded longerons, and formed circumferentials of aluminum alloy. With minor exceptions, flush rivets are used exclusively to attach the skin to the fuselage structure. There are three pressurized compartments: one in the forward part of the airplane, one aft of the rear bomb bay, and one in the extreme aft portion of the ship.

(1) The pilot, copilot, engineer, radio operator, navigator, and bombardier are stationed in the forward compartment and are provided with the following normal and emergency exits:

(a) Through the nose wheel well, by means of a hatch in the floor beside the engineer's station. Normal and emergency exit, normal entrance.

(b) Pressure bulkhead (218) door. Emergency exit through bomb bay.

(c) Engineer's removable window. Emergency exit while on ground or water only.

(2) The rear pressurized compartment is located immediately aft of the rear bomb bay and is connected with the forward compartment by a pressurized tunnel

Figure 2—Forward Compartment Entrance

Figure 3—Rear Entrance Door

which allows crew members access to either compartment during high altitude flight. Provisions for exit from the rear compartment are as follows:

(*a*) Pressure bulkhead (646) door. Emergency exit through aft bomb bay.

(*b*) Pressure bulkhead (834) door. Emergency exit to rear unpressurized compartment.

(3) Provisions for exit from the rear unpressurized compartment are as follows:

(*a*) Rear entrance door. Normal and emergency exits.

(*b*) Escape hatch on upper left side of fuselage. Emergency exit while on ground or water only.

(4) Pressure bulkheads, located at stations 1110 and 1144, form a small pressurized enclosure for the tail gunner. Entrance is gained through a door in the station 1110 bulkhead and emergency exit is made through a window at the tail gunner's right.

NOTE

When reference is made in this Handbook to certain locations in the airplane such as "Bulkhead 218," the No. "218" represents the distance in inches measured from the nose of the airplane to the station to which reference is made.

CAUTION

Any differential in pressure existing in the pressurized compartments must be equalized with outside pressure before an exit can be made. This is accomplished by pulling the cabin pressure release located at the left of the pilot, or on the right side wall of the fuselage at station 646.

e. LANDING GEAR.

(1) The main landing gear is a cantilever type, consisting of two air-oil shock strut assemblies, upon each of which are mounted two wheels with 56-inch tires. Retraction is accomplished electrically and an alternate motor is provided for emergency operation of the gear in the event of power or motor failure.

(2) The main landing-gear wheels are each equipped with expander tube-type hydraulic brakes, operated in the conventional manner from the rudder pedals.

CAUTION

After take-off, brakes should be applied before the start of wheel retraction.

f. NOSE GEAR.—The nose gear operates simultaneously with the main landing gear and consists of a trunnion, a compression strut, two torsion links, a universal assembly, a retracting mechanism, a single air-oil shock strut, and dual wheels equipped with 36-inch smooth tires. The wheel and axle assembly can turn through 360 degrees. Within 15 degrees each side of the center position, however, a cam and roller mechanism will return the gear to the center position. A towing lug is provided

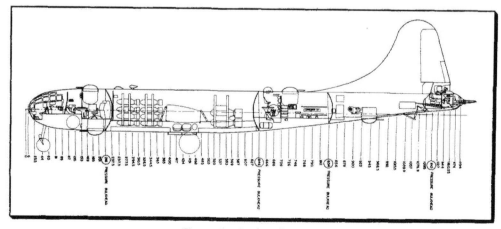

Figure 4—Stations Diagram

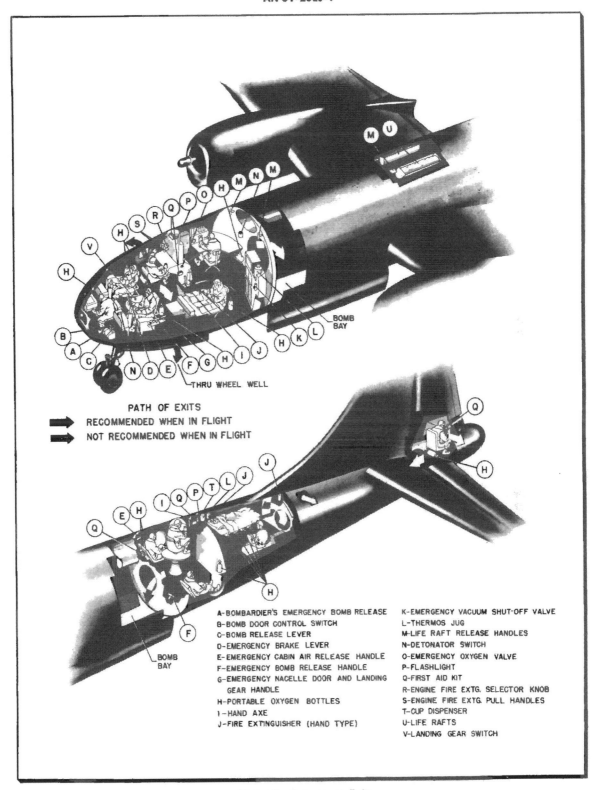

PATH OF EXITS

➡ RECOMMENDED WHEN IN FLIGHT

➡ NOT RECOMMENDED WHEN IN FLIGHT

A—BOMBARDIER'S EMERGENCY BOMB RELEASE
B—BOMB DOOR CONTROL SWITCH
C—BOMB RELEASE LEVER
D—EMERGENCY BRAKE LEVER
E—EMERGENCY CABIN AIR RELEASE HANDLE
F—EMERGENCY BOMB RELEASE HANDLE
G—EMERGENCY NACELLE DOOR AND LANDING
  GEAR HANDLE
H—PORTABLE OXYGEN BOTTLES
I—HAND AXE
J—FIRE EXTINGUISHER (HAND TYPE)

K—EMERGENCY VACUUM SHUT-OFF VALVE
L—THERMOS JUG
M—LIFE RAFT RELEASE HANDLES
N—DETONATOR SWITCH
O—EMERGENCY OXYGEN VALVE
P—FLASHLIGHT
Q—FIRST AID KIT
R—ENGINE FIRE EXTG. SELECTOR KNOB
S—ENGINE FIRE EXTG. PULL HANDLES
T—CUP DISPENSER
U—LIFE RAFTS
V—LANDING GEAR SWITCH

Figure 5—Emergency Exits

near the center of the axle assembly, and a shock absorber is mounted on the shock strut, to prevent wheel shimmy.

g. TAIL SKID.—A retractable tail skid operates in conjunction with the landing gear to prevent damage to the airplane in a tail-down landing.

2. POWER PLANT.

a. ENGINE.

(1) GENERAL.—The airplane is powered by four model R-3350-23 (B-29) or R-3350-21 (YB-29) Wright radial engines, which are geared, air-cooled, and have 18 cylinders with a displacement of 3,350 cubic inches. The reduction gear ratio from crankshaft to propeller is .350 (20:7).

(2) RATINGS.

(a) Take-off	2,200 brake horsepower at 2,800 revolutions per minute with 47.5 inches of mercury manifold pressure at sea level.
(b) Military Rated Power	2,200 brake horsepower at 2,600 revolutions per minute with 47.5 inches of mercury manifold pressure at 25,000 feet. Maximum duration 5 minutes.
(c) Normal Rated Power	2,000 brake horsepower at 2,400 revolutions per minute with 43.5 inches of mercury manifold pressure at 25,000 feet.

NOTE

Those airplanes equipped with R-3350-13, -21, and -23 engines not equipped with second order dampeners, referred to as "Model Test," should be operated in conformance with the following limitations:

Take-off rpm limited to 2600.

Maximum operational altitude of 15,000 feet.

Operation at maximum power should be held to the minimum coincident with safety.

(3) TEMPERATURE LIMITS.

Condition	Cylinder Head	Oil In
Ground Operation	260° C (500° F)	95° C (203° F)
Take-off Power	260° C (500° F)	95° C (203° F)
Military Power	260° C (500° F)	95° C (203°F)
Rated Power (1 hour)	248° C (475° F)	85° C (185° F)
Rated Power (cont)	232° C (450° F)	85° C (185° F)
70 percent Rated Power (cont)	232° C (450° F)	85° C (185° F)

b. PROPELLERS.—The four engines are fitted with Hamilton Standard, four-bladed, constant-speed, full-feathering propellers. Constant speed control is maintained with a governor and is operated electrically by four switches for individual control of each propeller. These switches are located on the aisle stand for use by the pilot.

c. TURBOSUPERCHARGERS.—Each engine is equipped with two type B-11 exhaust-driven turbosuperchargers mounted vertically on each side of the nacelle. The rpm of the turbine wheel is dependent on the position of the waste gate, which controls the amount of exhaust gases bypassed from the turbine nozzle box.

(1) M-H ELECTRONIC CONTROL SYSTEM.

(a) GENERAL.

1. The Minneapolis-Honeywell electronic turbosupercharger control system controls turbo boost on all four engines simultaneously from one manual control located on the pilot's aisle stand. The desired pressure may be selected to suit flight conditions by setting the control dial. The system automatically compensates for changes in atmospheric pressure by varying the speed of the turbosupercharger to maintain the manifold pressure selected. The primary sensing device for the system is the pressure trol, which measures induction system pressure at the carburetor intake and responds to variations by initiating a voltage signal. After being amplified by the turbo control amplifier, this signal causes rotation of the turbo waste gate motor. The motor adjusts the exhaust waste gate to increase or decrease turbosupercharger speed the exact amount necessary to effect the pressure change desired at the pressuretrol.

2. When the pilot wishes to reduce the manifold pressure on one or more engines for any reason, he may do so by retarding the corresponding throttle or throttles without lowering the selector dial setting. This gives him instant power in reserve for landing, for unequal engine powers if desired for maneuvering while in close formation, and power "cut-off" on any given engine if engine trouble should develop.

3. The control system includes a governor which protects the turbosupercharger from possible damage resulting from too rapid acceleration or overspeeding due to high altitude, duct failure, or sudden throttle manipulation. At high altitude, a condition may be reached where further advancing the dial setting will not produce an increase in manifold pressure. This will indicate that the overspeed portion of the governor is functioning to limit turbo speed to safe values. When this condition is reached, the dial should be turned down (counterclockwise) to the point where it can again control manifold pressure.

CAUTION

Do not use red-lined dial settings from 8 to 10 except in cases of extreme emergency. High manifold pressures obtained with the dial set in this range cause severe engine stress and should not be maintained for more than 2 minutes.

4. The system is supplied 115-volt, 400-cycle alternating current through a 5-ampere fuse in the radio compass relay shield located above the radio operator's table.

(b) INDUCTION SYSTEM PRESSURETROL.—One pressuretrol is mounted in each nacelle on the left-hand side of the intercooler.

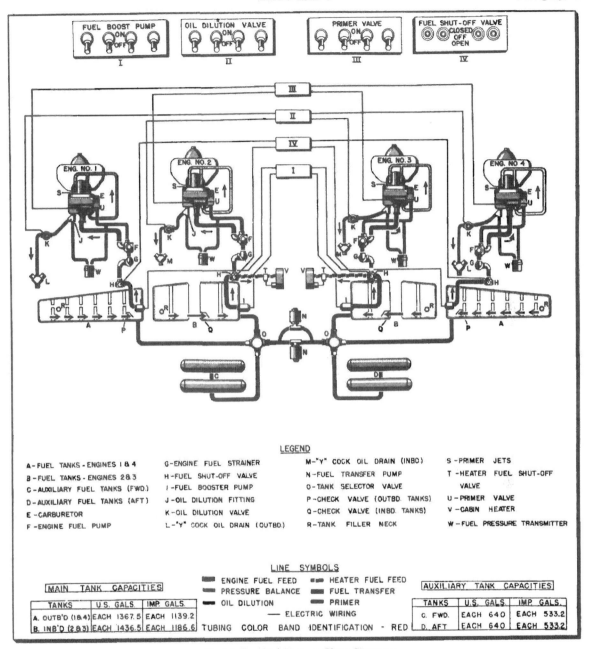

Figure 6—Fuel System Flow Diagram

(c) TURBO CONTROL AMPLIFIERS.—The four amplifier units, one for each nacelle, are located, two above and two below, the navigator's table. Each amplifier is supplied with its own plate voltage power supply so that failure of its power supply will affect only one amplifier and control system.

(d) WASTE GATE MOTOR.—The motor which operates the waste gate is a two-phase unit capable of rotation in either direction, depending on the phase rela-

tion of the current passed by the amplifier. Motor rotation is transmitted through a gear train and linkage to position the waste gate.

(e) TURBO GOVERNOR.—The turbo governor automatically causes the waste gate to open when the turbine is accelerating too rapidly or when the maximum safe speed (26,400 rpm at 35,000 feet) is reached.

(f) TURBO BOOST SELECTOR.—Turbo boost pressures are selected by setting the dial on the turbo boost selector. The divisions on the dial from "0 to 8" are used to select the desired manifold pressure for take-off, climbing, cruising, and gliding. A dial setting of "8" provides the turbo boost which will allow maximum take-off power at all altitudes up to that at which over-speed control occurs. A dial stop prevents dial rotation into the emergency power range beyond "8" unless the dial stop release is pressed to the right. The calibration potentiometers in the turbo boost selector are synchronized so that identical manifold pressures on all engines will be obtained for a given dial setting when rpm of all engines are synchronized.

d. COWL FLAPS.

(1) Cowl flaps are installed on each nacelle to regulate the cooling of the engines, and are electrically controlled through toggle switches on the engineer's switch panel. Thermocouples on each engine, which are connected to indicators on the engineer's instrument panel, indicate the cylinder head temperature of each engine, permitting the engineer to regulate the cowl flaps for the desired temperature. Positioning of the cowl flaps is shown by an indicator on the engineer's instrument panel.

(2) Cowl flaps should be open for start, warm-up, and taxying, and should be closed while engine is feathered. In all other operating conditions the cowl flap position will be determined by maximum and minimum cylinder head temperature allowable for these conditions.

NOTE

Closing the cowl flaps during starting operations does not speed engine warm-up and is harmful to the engine. Cowl flaps should be fully open for all ground operation except take-off and landing.

e. AUTOMATIC ENGINE CONTROL. — Should engine control cables be severed, the throttles will automatically assume the fully opened position, and the supercharger waste gates will stay as set. Should the lever arrangement between the waste gate motor and waste gates be severed, the supercharger waste gates will assume the *"full open"* position.

f. FUEL SYSTEM.

(1) Each engine receives its fuel supply from a system which is independent of the other three engines. Each outboard engine is fed from a series of seven, interconnected, self-sealing cells with a total net capacity of 1367.5 U. S. (1138.9 Imperial) gallons. Each inboard engine is supplied from an individual tank assembly consisting of four interconnected cells with a capacity of 1436.5 U. S. (1196.4 Imperial) gallons. Four releasable auxiliary tanks may be installed, two in each bomb bay, in place of bombs, adding 2560 U. S. (2132.5 Imperial) gallons to the total amount of gasoline which may be carried. The total capacity of the wing tanks and auxiliary tanks is 8168 U. S. (6803 Imperial) gallons. The fuel in the auxiliary tanks must be transferred to the main engine tanks when it is required, as it cannot be used directly from the auxiliary tanks.

(2) The engine fuel pumps are type G-10 and are powered directly from the fuel pump drives on the engines. An electric motor-driven booster pump is provided for each fuel tank and is located at each tank outlet. These pumps are used to supplement the fuel pumps in starting and take-off to prevent vapor lock at high altitudes and to provide fuel in case of engine-driven pump failure. Boost pumps are controlled at low speed and fixed pressure of 8 pounds per square inch by switches on the engineer's switch panel. Further control is provided by four rheostats on the engineer's switch panel giving a range of 12 to 18 pounds per square inch.

WARNING

If an engine-driven fuel pump fails and the boost pump is used to supply fuel pressure, the turbosupercharger should not be operated. Since fuel boost pressure will not increase with carburetor duct pressure, a dangerously lean mixture will result causing detonation.

(3) The fuel may be transferred from one tank to another by means of two reversible, electric motor-driven pumps mounted under the midwing section between the bomb bays, and controlled by switches on the engineer's switch panel. The tanks are interconnected with self-sealing hose, and selection of transfer between tanks is accomplished by two cable controlled selector valves which may be adjusted by levers at the engineer's stand.

NOTE

Fuel may be transferred only across the center line of the airplane. Thus it is necessary in transferring from one adjacent wing tank to another, to first transfer the fuel to the opposite side of the airplane and then back to the tank desired.

(4) When in doubt as to whether a transfer can be made, always remember that *both selector levers* must be set to the desired tanks. If both tanks appear on the same lever, it is obvious that two transfers are required. See figure 7 for the proper procedure for transferring fuel.

(5) Four switches on the engineer's switch panel control the engine priming solenoid valves, which allow fuel to be directed from the carburetor to the engine blower case. The fuel boost pumps must be "ON" to supply fuel under pressure to the carburetor before priming.

g. OIL SYSTEM.

(1) Each engine receives its oil supply from an 85 U. S. (70.8 Imperial) gallons self-sealing tank, located in the nacelle rear. An oil cooler is located in the oil "OUT" line between each engine and oil tank. The air flow through the oil cooler is controlled automatically by a temperature regulator or may be manually regulated by means of switches on the engineer's switch panel, if desired.

(2) The oil may be diluted with gasoline at the end of a flight, if low temperatures are anticipated. Four switches mounted on the engineer's switch panel operate the four solenoid valves which control dilution of the oil.

DIRECT TRANSFER CAN BE MADE ONLY BETWEEN TANKS DESIGNATED AT OPPOSITE LEVERS. (EXAMPLES 1 & 2)

SHOULD A TRANSFER BE DESIRED BETWEEN TWO TANKS DESIGNATED AT ONE LEVER IT IS NECESSARY TO FIRST TRANSFER THE FUEL TO ONE OF THE TANKS DESIGNATED AT THE OPPOSITE LEVER, THEN BACK TO THE DESIRED TANK. (EXAMPLES 3 & 4)

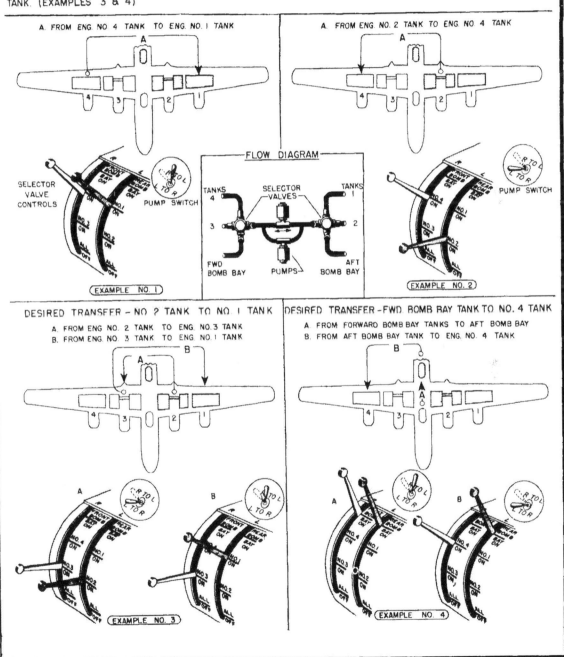

Figure 7—Fuel Transfer Operation Diagram

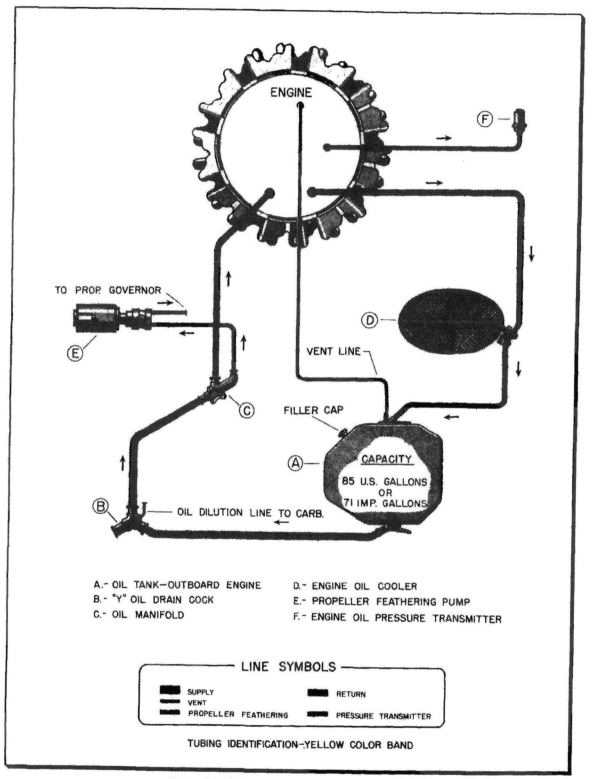

ENGINE

F

TO PROP. GOVERNOR

E

C

VENT LINE

D

FILLER CAP

A

CAPACITY

85 U.S. GALLONS
OR
71 IMP. GALLONS

B

OIL DILUTION LINE TO CARB.

A.- OIL TANK—OUTBOARD ENGINE
B.- "Y" OIL DRAIN COCK
C.- OIL MANIFOLD

D.- ENGINE OIL COOLER
E.- PROPELLER FEATHERING PUMP
F.- ENGINE OIL PRESSURE TRANSMITTER

LINE SYMBOLS

SUPPLY
VENT
PROPELLER FEATHERING

RETURN

PRESSURE TRANSMITTER

TUBING IDENTIFICATION—YELLOW COLOR BAND

Figure 8—Oil Flow Diagram—Engines 1 and 4

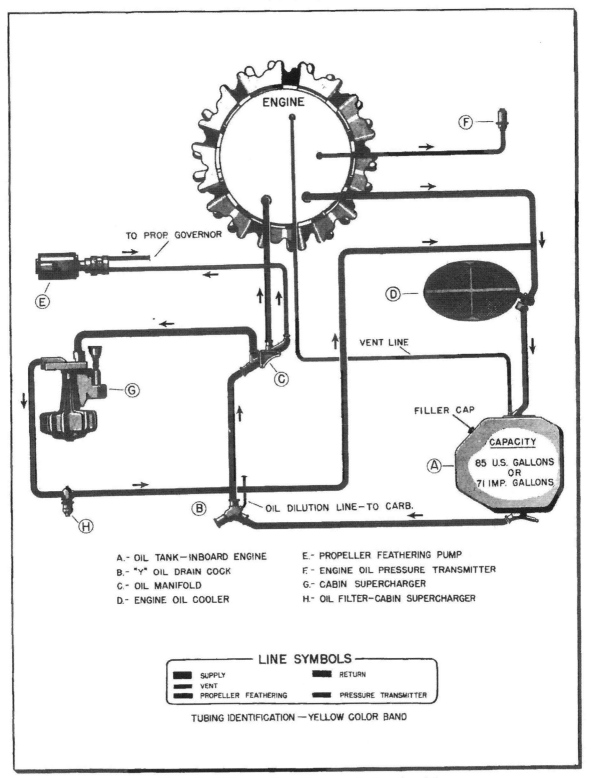

A.- OIL TANK—INBOARD ENGINE
B.- "Y" OIL DRAIN COCK
C.- OIL MANIFOLD
D.- ENGINE OIL COOLER

E.- PROPELLER FEATHERING PUMP
F.- ENGINE OIL PRESSURE TRANSMITTER
G.- CABIN SUPERCHARGER
H.- OIL FILTER—CABIN SUPERCHARGER

LINE SYMBOLS

SUPPLY   RETURN
VENT
PROPELLER FEATHERING   PRESSURE TRANSMITTER

TUBING IDENTIFICATION — YELLOW COLOR BAND

Figure 9—Oil System Flow Diagram—Engines 2 and 3

(3) Engine oil is also used in the operation of the cabin superchargers which are geared to engine Nos. 2 and 3.

3. CONTROLS.

a. LOCATION OF CONTROLS.

(1) GENERAL.—Controls on this airplane do not differ greatly from conventional designs, except, that the pilot and copilot have been relieved of the majority of the power plant controls and most of the basic mechanical and electrical system operations, so that they may concentrate on flying technique and combat strategy. This has been accomplished by supplying the engineer with a separate station complete with all the instruments and controls required. The engineer is located on the right side of the airplane behind the copilot, facing aft. This places him in close communication at all times with the pilot and copilot and also enables him to visually check all four engines while seated at his station. The throttle levers are triplicated, one set each being available for the pilot, copilot, and engineer. The pilot, however, may at any time override the engineer's throttle controls to maintain sole command. The turbosuperchargers are all controlled by a single dial knob on the pilot's aisle stand.

(2) PILOT'S AND COPILOT'S CONTROL STANDS.—The pilot and copilot are each provided with a control stand upon which the power plant control levers are mounted. Controls for the trim tabs are also provided at these stations. The throttle warning reset buttons are located on the copilot's control stand and the landing-gear power transfer switch and the emergency cabin pressure, bomb, and landing-gear releases are mounted on the pilot's stand.

(3) ENGINEER'S CONTROL STAND.—The engineer's control stand provides controls for the throttles, mixture, fuel transfer, cabin supercharger, and vacuum selector. The engineer's switch panel is located immediately aft of the control stand. (See figure 13.)

(4) AISLE STAND.—A stand is provided in the aisle between the pilot and copilot, allowing each easy access to the controls. Controls located here consist of the control surface lock lever, emergency brake levers, wing flap control switch, propeller feathering switches, emergency alarm switch, phone call switch, formation light rheostat, position light switches, identification light switches, propeller rpm, propeller pitch circuit breaker resets, A.F.C.E. system controls, and turbo boost selector.

b. OPERATION OF CONTROLS.

(1) FLIGHT CONTROLS.

(a) AILERON, ELEVATOR, AND RUDDER CONTROLS.—The ailerons, elevators, rudder, and all trim tabs have the conventional system of controls. The control surfaces are locked simultaneously by a single control located on the aisle stand.

(b) WING FLAPS.—The wing flaps are actuated by power transmitted from a reversible electric motor through twin screw mechanisms in each wing which are connected to the flap torque tubes. The flaps travel on track and roller mechanisms in such a manner that the flaps extend beyond the trailing edge of the wing as they are lowered. The flaps are lowered 45 degrees for landing and 25 degrees to assist in taking off. The flap control switch is installed on the pilot's aisle stand and the position indicator is mounted on the copilot's instrument panel. In cases of emergency due to power or motor failure, the flaps may be operated by a portable electric motor normally stowed on the upper wing surface of the inboard wing, approximately on the center line of the airplane. The motor is engaged with a torque connection on the top of the midwing section between the bomb bays, and the electric receptacle is located adjacent to the torque connection.

CAUTION

To operate the portable motor from the above-mentioned receptacle, either the landing-gear power transfer switch (pilot's control stand) or the emergency circuit switch (battery solenoid shield) must be in the "EMERGENCY POSITION."

WARNING

Do not lower wing flaps or fly the airplane with wing flaps full down at a speed in excess of 180 miles per hour or with the flaps half down (25 degrees) above 220 miles per hour.

(c) A.F.C.E. SYSTEM.—Controls for operation of this equipment are mounted on the aisle stand. Telltale lights indicate when servo motors are in operation.

CAUTION

Do not turn on A.F.C.E.S. motors while any telltale light is burning steadily.

(2) ENGINE CONTROLS.

(a) IGNITION SWITCHES.

Description: Rotary levers, type B-5 ignition switches.

Location: Engineer's instrument panel.

Function: Provide individual engine ignition control, utilizing either or both circuits of the dual-type magnetos.

(b) CONTROL LEVERS.

1. THROTTLE.

Description: Three throttle control levers for each engine interconnected by cables.

Location: Pilot's control stand, copilot's control stand, and engineer's control stand.

Function: To provide control of the throttles.

2. SUPERCHARGER CONTROL.

Description: One dial knob on turbo boost control.

Location: Pilot's aisle stand.

Function: Provides simultaneous control of all turbosuperchargers and turbo boost.

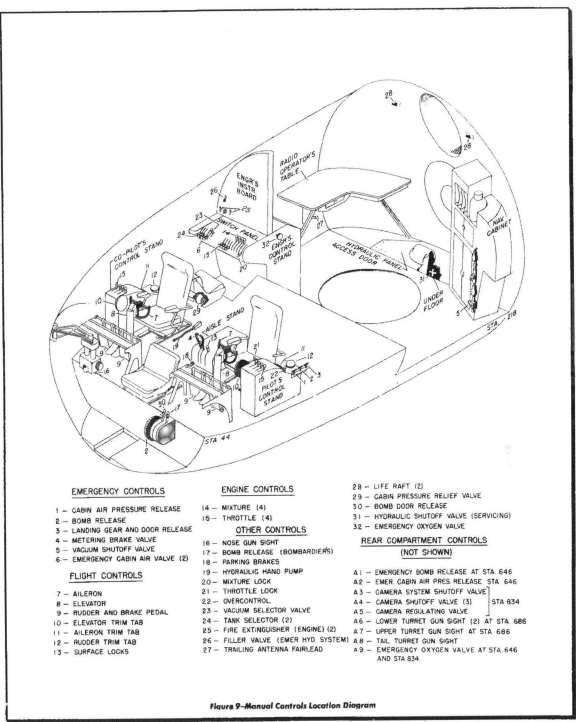

EMERGENCY CONTROLS

1 — CABIN AIR PRESSURE RELEASE
2 — BOMB RELEASE
3 — LANDING GEAR AND DOOR RELEASE
4 — METERING BRAKE VALVE
5 — VACUUM SHUTOFF VALVE
6 — EMERGENCY CABIN AIR VALVE (2)

FLIGHT CONTROLS

7 — AILERON
8 — ELEVATOR
9 — RUDDER AND BRAKE PEDAL
10 — ELEVATOR TRIM TAB
11 — AILERON TRIM TAB
12 — RUDDER TRIM TAB
13 — SURFACE LOCKS

ENGINE CONTROLS

14 — MIXTURE (4)
15 — THROTTLE (4)

OTHER CONTROLS

16 — NOSE GUN SIGHT
17 — BOMB RELEASE (BOMBARDIER'S)
18 — PARKING BRAKES
19 — HYDRAULIC HAND PUMP
20 — MIXTURE LOCK
21 — THROTTLE LOCK
22 — OVERCONTROL
23 — VACUUM SELECTOR VALVE
24 — TANK SELECTOR (2)
25 — FIRE EXTINGUISHER (ENGINE) (2)
26 — FILLER VALVE (EMER. HYD. SYSTEM)
27 — TRAILING ANTENNA FAIRLEAD

28 — LIFE RAFT (2)
29 — CABIN PRESSURE RELIEF VALVE
30 — BOMB DOOR RELEASE
31 — HYDRAULIC SHUTOFF VALVE (SERVICING)
32 — EMERGENCY OXYGEN VALVE

REAR COMPARTMENT CONTROLS
(NOT SHOWN)

A1 — EMERGENCY BOMB RELEASE AT STA. 646
A2 — EMER. CABIN AIR PRES. RELEASE STA. 646
A3 — CAMERA SYSTEM SHUTOFF VALVE
A4 — CAMERA SHUTOFF VALVE (3)   STA. 834
A5 — CAMERA REGULATING VALVE
A6 — LOWER TURRET GUN SIGHT (2) AT STA. 686
A7 — UPPER TURRET GUN SIGHT AT STA. 686
A8 — TAIL TURRET GUN SIGHT
A9 — EMERGENCY OXYGEN VALVE AT STA. 646
AND STA. 834

Figure 9—Manual Controls Location Diagram

Figure 10—Manual Controls Location Diagram

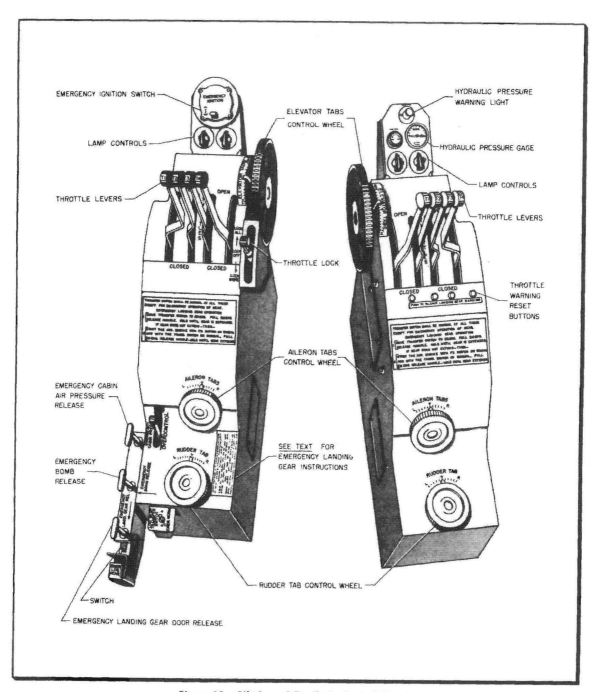

EMERGENCY IGNITION SWITCH

LAMP CONTROLS

ELEVATOR TABS
CONTROL WHEEL

THROTTLE LEVERS

HYDRAULIC PRESSURE
WARNING LIGHT

HYDRAULIC PRESSURE GAGE

LAMP CONTROLS

THROTTLE LEVERS

THROTTLE LOCK

THROTTLE
WARNING
RESET
BUTTONS

EMERGENCY CABIN
AIR PRESSURE
RELEASE

AILERON TABS
CONTROL WHEEL

EMERGENCY
BOMB
RELEASE

SEE TEXT FOR
EMERGENCY LANDING
GEAR INSTRUCTIONS

SWITCH

RUDDER TAB CONTROL WHEEL

EMERGENCY LANDING GEAR DOOR RELEASE

Figure 11—Pilot's and Copilot's Control Stands

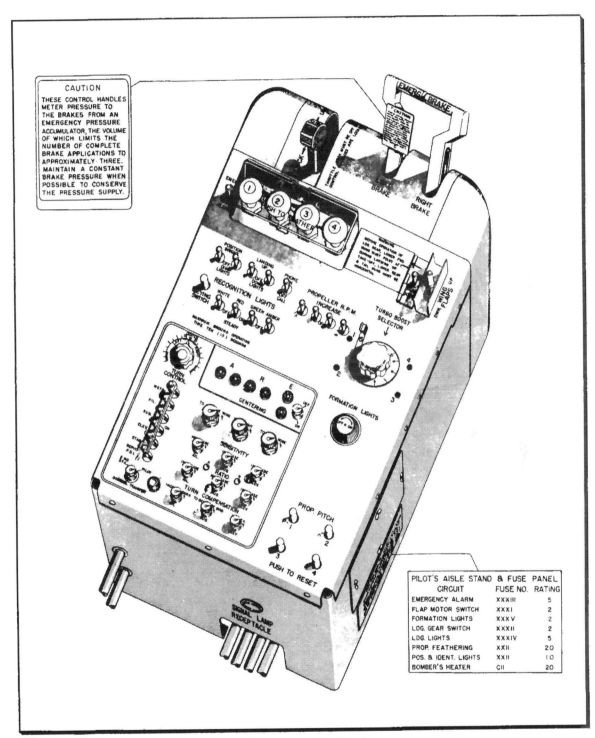

CAUTION

THESE CONTROL HANDLES
METER PRESSURE TO
THE BRAKES FROM AN
EMERGENCY PRESSURE
ACCUMULATOR, THE VOLUME
OF WHICH LIMITS THE
NUMBER OF COMPLETE
BRAKE APPLICATIONS TO
APPROXIMATELY THREE.
MAINTAIN A CONSTANT
BRAKE PRESSURE WHEN
POSSIBLE TO CONSERVE
THE PRESSURE SUPPLY.

PILOT'S AISLE STAND & FUSE PANEL		
CIRCUIT	FUSE NO.	RATING
EMERGENCY ALARM	XXXIII	5
FLAP MOTOR SWITCH	XXXI	2
FORMATION LIGHTS	XXXV	2
LDG. GEAR SWITCH	XXXII	2
LDG. LIGHTS	XXXIV	5
PROP. FEATHERING	XXII	20
POS. & IDENT. LIGHTS	XXII	10
BOMBER'S HEATER	CII	20

Figure 12—Aisle Stand

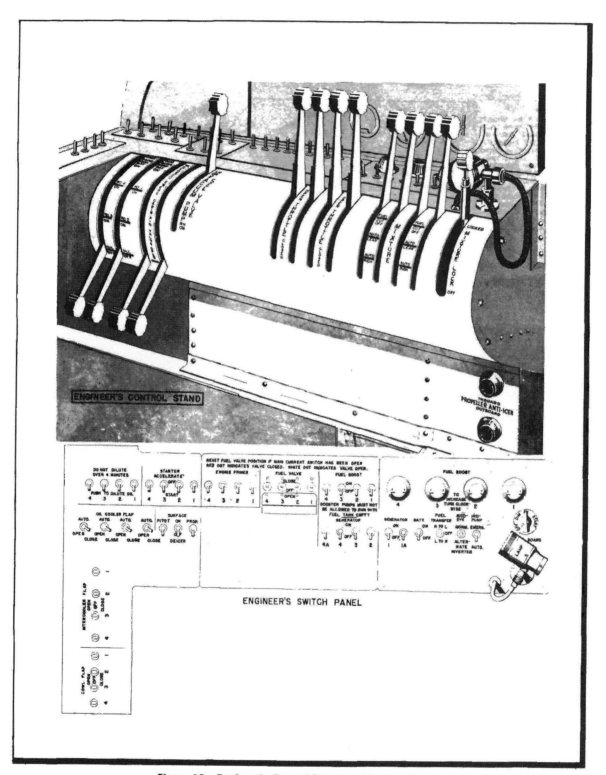

Figure 13—Engineer's Control Stand and Switch Panel

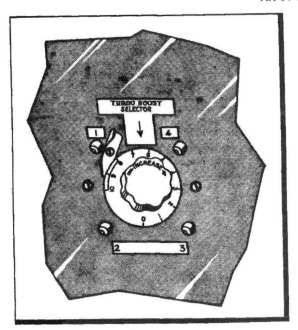

Figure 14—Turbo Boost Selector

3. SUPERCHARGER SYNCHRONIZATION.

Description: Four calibration screws.

Location: Under four screw caps on pilot's aisle stand.

Function: Adjust the correlation of four manifold pressures to a single dial setting.

4. MIXTURE CONTROL.

Description: Control levers connected to each carburetor mixture control by cables.

Location: Engineer's stand.

Function: Provide control of the carburetor mixture.

5. MIXTURE LOCK.

Description: Control lever.
Location: Engineer's stand.
Function: Apply varying degrees of friction.

6. OVERCONTROL.

Description: Control lever.
Location: Pilot's control stand.
Function: Allows the pilot, in emergencies, to assume control over the engineer's throttle levers.

(c) COWL FLAP SWITCHES.

Description: Four, momentary contact switches.
Location: Engineer's switch panel.
Function: Provide control of the cylinder-head temperature by operating the cowl flaps.

(d) INTERCOOLER SWITCHES.

Description: Four momentary contact switches.
Location: Engineer's switch panel.
Function: Provide control of the carburetor air temperature.

(e) OIL COOLER SWITCHES.

Description: Four, three-position switches: "OPEN," "CLOSED," or "AUTO."
Location: Engineer's switch panel.
Function: Provide control of the oil temperature. The oil cooler exit is governed automatically by a thermostat when in the "AUTO" position.

(f) PRIMER SWITCHES.

Description: Four, momentary contact switches.
Location: Engineer's switch panel.
Function: Operate solenoid valves located in each nacelle, directing fuel to the engine blower cases, thus facilitating starting.

(g) OIL DILUTION SWITCHES.

Description: Four, momentary contact switches.
Location: Engineer's switch panel.
Function: Operate the solenoid valves allowing fuel to dilute the engine oil to facilitate cold weather starting.

(h) FUEL SUPPLY.

1. FUEL BOOST SWITCHES.

Description: Four, toggle switches.
Location: Engineer's switch panel.
Function: Operate the fuel boost pumps which supply fuel to the carburetors from each fuel system during starting. The boost pumps are also used to augment the fuel pumps during take-off and operation above 15,000 feet.

2. FUEL BOOST RHEOSTATS.

Description: Four rheostats.
Location: Engineer's panel.
Function: Control the amount of fuel pressure from the boost pumps.

CAUTION

Fuel pressure must not exceed 18 pounds per square inch.

3. FUEL SHUT-OFF SWITCHES.

Description: Four, momentary contact switches.
Location: Engineer's switch panel.
Function: Provide control of the solenoid operated fuel shut-off valve. Two opposed solenoids are used; one is employed for closing, the other for the opening action. Small dots near each switch indicate the direction in which the valve was last actuated. A transparent shield protects the switches from accidental operation.

4. FUEL TANK SELECTOR LEVERS.

Description: Two control levers.
Location: Left side of engineer's control stand.
Function: Operate by means of cables, the two selector valves located under the midwing section. Four positions are available on each selector valve to permit choice of tanks, when transferring fuel.

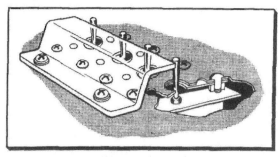

Figure 15—Fuel Shut-off Valve

5. FUEL TRANSFER PUMP SWITCH.

Description: Three-pole, triple-throw switch.

Location: Engineer's switch panel.

Function: Provide control of the fuel transfer pumps. Three positions, "L to R," "R to L," and "OFF" are indicated. The pump switch is interlocked with the selector valves by a relay and prevents the pump from operating should the selector valve be off center.

6. FUEL AND OIL QUANTITY GAGE SELECTOR KNOBS.

Description: Two, four-position selector knobs.

Location: Engineer's instrument panel, one knob each for the fuel and oil gages.

Function: Allow choice of indication of the quantities in any of the engine fuel tanks and oil tanks.

(i) PROPELLER CONTROLS.

1. PILOT'S PROPELLER SWITCHES.

Description: Four, momentary contact switches. These switches operate in conjunction with amber signal lights in the copilot's instrument panel. The signal lights indicate the limit of governor travel in either direction.

Location: Pilot's aisle stand.

Function: Provide individual control of the propellers.

2. FEATHERING SWITCHES.

Description: Four, magnetic, push-button switches which, when operated, are held engaged by the magnetic holding feature until feathering is complete.

Location: Aisle stand.

Function and Operation: Close the circuit to the propeller feathering pump. Should it be desired to stop the action prior to completion, the buttons may be pulled out manually. Propeller unfeathering requires that the buttons be manually engaged, since the operation requires oil pressures in excess of that at which the magnetic holding feature ceases to function. The button should be held engaged until the propeller has attained sufficient rotation (200 rpm) for the governor to assume control. A transparent, hinged guard protects the push buttons from accidental operation.

3. PROPELLER ANTI-ICER SWITCH.

Description: Toggle switch.

Location: Engineer's switch panel.

Function: Operate the electrical pumps which supply anti-icing fluid to the propellers.

4. PROPELLER ANTI-ICER RHEOSTAT.

Description: Two control knobs.

Location: Lower inboard portion of the engineer's stand.

Function: Varies the rate of propeller anti-icer fluid from 2 gallons per hour to 5 gallons per hour. One rheostat controls flow to the outboard propellers and the other to the inboard propellers.

(j) STARTER SWITCHES.

Description: Four, momentary contact switches.

Location: Engineer's switch panel.

Function: Energize and mesh starters for engine start. Three positions, "OFF," "ACCELERATE," and "START" are provided for each of the four starter switches.

(k) ENGINE FIRE EXTINGUISHER.

1. SELECTOR KNOB.

Description: Manually operated, four-position knob.

Figure 16—Fuel and Oil Quantity Gage Selector Knobs

Location: Engineer's instrument board.

Function: Selection of one of the four engines to which to direct the CO_2 discharge.

WARNING

Do not try to distribute the discharge from one bottle to more than one engine, as the capacity of a single bottle will not be sufficient for effective use on more than one engine.

2. RELEASE HANDLES.

Description: Two, manually operated pull handles, one for each of the two CO_2 charge bottles.

Figure 17—Forward Pressurized Compartment

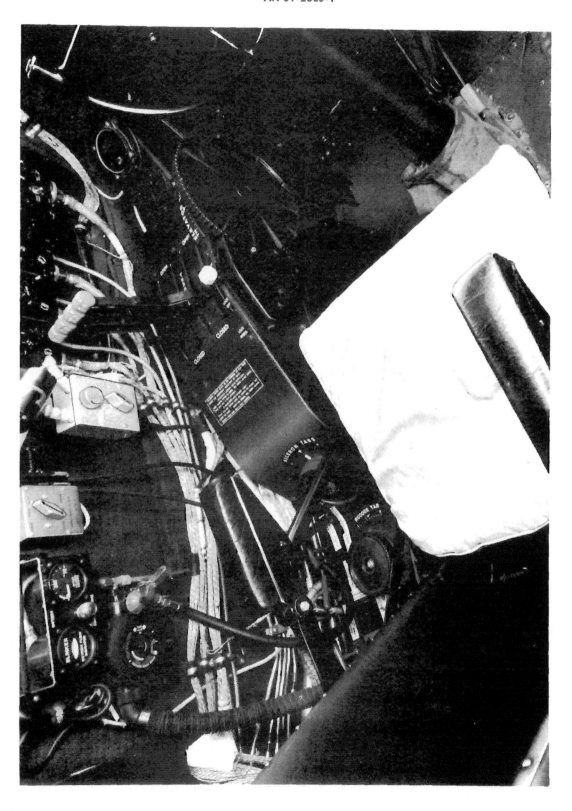

Figure 18—Pilot's Station

Figure 19—Copilot's Station

Location: Engineer's instrument panel.

Function: Release of CO_2 discharge to the desired engine.

(3) HYDRAULIC SYSTEM CONTROLS.

(a) BRAKE PEDALS.

Description: Standard type rudder pedals.

Location: Pilot's and copilot's stations.

Function: Provide control in taxying by tilting the rudder pedals forward for brake action. Each right and left brake may be controlled independently.

WARNING

Repeated, excessive use of brakes without sufficient cooling intervals between applications, will cause dangerous overheating and could result in failure of the brake structure or the wheels and the blowing of tires. Avoid needlessly short stops especially from high speeds and the dragging of brakes while taxying. After take-off apply brakes before retracting wheels.

(b) EMERGENCY BRAKE LEVERS.

Description: Two lever handles.

Location: Aisle stand.

Function: Provide individual or dual metering, as conditions warrant.

WARNING

Should conditions arise whereby it is necessary to use the emergency system during a landing, care must be taken not to "meter" the brakes excessively, as this may drain the pressure in the emergency accumulator to a point where the pressure is exhausted before the landing is completed.

Figure 20—Parking Brake Handle

(c) PARKING BRAKE HANDLE.

Description: Button-type pull handle.

Location: Pilot's rudder pedal stand, upper right.

Function: Set parking brakes. Operate foot brakes, then pull out the parking brake handle. This locks the metering valves in the depressed position.

CAUTION

Do not apply parking brake until drums are cool.

(d) PUMP SWITCH.

Description: Toggle switch.

Location: Engineer's switch panel.

Function: For emergency or service override of regulator ("ON" position only as it will not cut off motor).

(e) HAND PUMP.

Description: Handle.

Location: Left of the copilot's seat, on the floor.

Function: Provide pressure for setting the parking brakes.

(f) FILLER VALVE, EMERGENCY SYSTEM.

Description: Two-way hydraulic valve.

Location: Engineer's instrument board.

Function: Charge the emergency hydraulic accumulator. The valve is normally closed when the emergency system pressure is at its maximum.

(g) SERVICE SHUT-OFF VALVE.

Description: Hand-operated screw-type valve.

Location: On hydraulic panel under the pilot's compartment floor, at bulkhead 218.

Function: Drain the service system pressure back to the supply tank.

(4) LANDING-GEAR CONTROLS.

(a) LANDING-GEAR SWITCH.

Description: Toggle switch.

Location: Aisle stand.

Function: Provide control of regular nose gear and landing-gear (including nacelle doors) retracting motors.

(b) LANDING-GEAR POWER TRANSFER SWITCH.

Description: Toggle switch.

Location: Pilot's control stand.

Function: Disconnect the power from the normal landing-gear operators and connect the emergency power bus to the main power system, should operation of the emergency landing gear, bomb door, or wing flap motors with normal power be desired.

NOTE

THE FOLLOWING ARE EMERGENCY PROVISIONS—READ CAREFULLY.

Figure 21—Engineer's Station

(c) EMERGENCY LANDING-GEAR SWITCH
AND DOOR RELEASE HANDLE.

Description: T-type pull handle and toggle switch.

Location: Aft portion of the pilot's control stand.

Function and Operation: Open the nacelle wheel doors by mechanically releasing the screw and allowing the doors to fall open. Initial travel of the handle releases the nacelle doors. Subsequent travel engages a momentary switch, which operates to lower out successively, the nose gear, left main landing gear, and right main landing gear.

WARNING

The pull handle must be held pulled out until the lowering operation is complete. Check position of landing gear visually!

NOTE

The emergency motors may be used to retract the landing gear in the same order, by holding the emergency gear switch (aft of the release handle) depressed in the "UP" position. No means are provided for emergency retraction of the nacelle doors.

To operate the emergency landing-gear motors, either the landing-gear power transfer switch (pilot's control stand) or the emergency circuit switch (battery solenoid shield) must be in the "EMERGENCY" position.

Figure 22—Throttle Warning Reset Buttons

(d) WARNING RESET BUTTONS.

Description: Four, plunger-type buttons.

Location: Copilot's control stand, to the rear of the throttle levers.

Function and Operation: Shut off the warning horn which sounds when the throttle is closed while the landing gear is retracted. Depression of the button for the throttle in question, disengages a spacer and allows the switch to open the horn circuit. However, if the throttle lever is then advanced from the "CLOSED" position, the button will return to the operating position.

(5) CABIN HEATING AND SUPERCHARGER CONTROLS.

(a) CABIN AIRFLOW VALVE CONTROL LEVERS.

Description: Two levers.

Location: Engineer's control stand.

Function: Shut off ventilating ducts by holding vent check valves, located in the ventilating duct at the inlet to the communication tunnel, in "CLOSED" position.

(b) CABIN HEATING SWITCHES.

Description: Two toggle switches.

Location: Engineer's auxiliary switch panel.

Function: Operate either or both cabin heating systems.

(c) MANUAL PRESSURE RELIEF VALVE.

Description: Adjustable spring-loaded valve.

Location: Under the outboard edge of the engineer's seat.

Function: Allow the engineer to manually control the cabin pressure regulators, or to release the cabin pressure at high altitudes when combat conditions are anticipated.

(d) EMERGENCY PRESSURE RELEASE HANDLES.

Description: Two, T-type pull handles.

Location: One on the pilot's control stand and the other on the right side wall of rear pressurized compartment, near the forward bulkhead.

Function: Permit rapid escape of air from the pressurized cabin and allow the pressure bulkhead doors to be opened in an emergency.

(e) PRESSURE WARNING SHUT-OFF SWITCH.

Description: Single throw toggle switch.

Location: Engineer's auxiliary switch panel.

Function: Disconnect the cabin pressure warning horn should operation above 12,000 feet cabin altitude be contemplated.

(6) VACUUM SYSTEM CONTROLS.

(a) VACUUM SELECTOR LEVER.

Description: Lever handle.

Location: Engineer's control stand.

Function: Permit selection of either the right or left inboard engine vacuum pump to supply suction for operating the gyro instruments.

(b) EMERGENCY SHUT-OFF VALVE.

Description: Two-position, manually operated valve.

Location: Front of the navigator's cabinet.

Function: Isolate de-icing system and camera vacuum lines from the vacuum system in case of damage to de-icer boots or lines.

(c) CAMERA VACUUM SHUT-OFF VALVE
(MASTER).

Description: Two-position, manually operated valve.

Location: Camera panel, station 834.

Function: Isolate camera vacuum system from the main vacuum system.

CAUTION

This shut-off valve must be open at all times to supply vacuum to the de-icers. Otherwise, there is danger that the de-icers may flutter due to the air flow over the leading edges.

(d) CAMERA VACUUM SHUT-OFF VALVES
(INDIVIDUAL).

Description: Three, two-position manually operated valves.

Location: Camera panel, station 834.

Function: Shut off vacuum in each of the three individual camera vacuum lines.

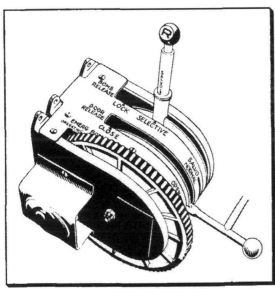

Figure 23—Bomb Controls

(7) BOMB CONTROLS.

(a) RELEASE CONTROL.

Description: Manually operated lever.

Location: Left of the bombardier's seat.

Function: Allow choice of the positions, "LOCK," "SELECTIVE," and "SALVO," in controlling the individual bomb release units. A pin on the bomb door control lever projects in the path of the bomb release lever and prevents salvo release of the bombs with the doors closed. Conversely, the doors cannot be closed while there is any possibility of bombs being dropped.

(b) RELEASE SWITCH.

Description: Momentary contact switch. A hinged guard on the switch provides protection against accidental release.

Location: On the floor to the left of the bombardier's seat.

Function: Initiate the electrical release of bombs.

(c) INTERVAL RELEASE.

Description: Control box.

Location: Bombardier's instrument panel.

Function: Provide pulses for either selective or train release of bombs. Controls are provided to vary the number and interval of bombs in a train.

(d) EMERGENCY RELEASE.

1. BOMBARDIER'S RELEASE AND
REWIND WHEEL.

Description: Handwheel.

Location: Left of the bombardier's seat.

Function: Effect emergency release of the bombs and rewind the emergency system after release has been accomplished.

Operation: Two and one-half turns clockwise are necessary to open the doors and release all bombs. The same number of turns in the opposite direction completely rewinds the system.

2. BOMB RELEASE PULL HANDLES.

Description: Two, T-type cable pull handles.

Location: One on the aft end of the pilot's control stand, and the other at the forward bulkhead in the rear pressurized compartment on the left side near the communication tunnel.

Function: Effect emergency release of all bombs.

Operation: Approximately 30 inches of travel is necessary to complete the release. By means of cables the pull handle operates the bomb coordinating unit, which is a mechanism designed to transmit the first portion of the pull to the bomb door emergency releases. Subsequent cable pull is directed to the bomb release levers which drop the bombs unarmed. A safeguard against any bombs being released before the doors are fully opened is provided by an interlock system which locks the release levers until the doors reach their open position.

(e) GROUP SELECTOR SWITCHES.

Description: Four toggle switches.

Location: Bombardier's instrument panel.

Function: Allow the bombardier to remove any or all of the bomb groups from the normal (layer) release sequence.

(f) TANK SAFETY SWITCH.

Description: Two toggle switches.

Location: One switch in the left front third of each bomb bay, above the catwalk.

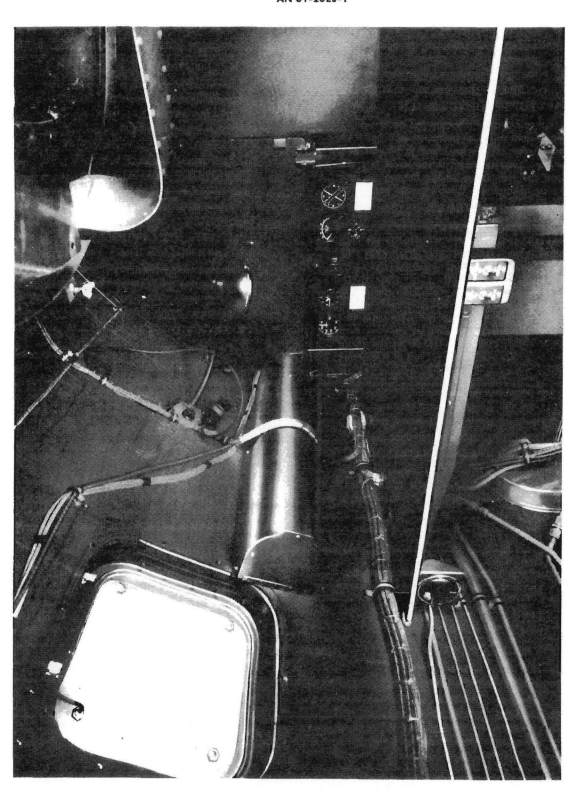

Figure 24—Navigator's Station

Function: Open the electrical release circuits as a safety feature when the bomb bay tanks are installed.

(g) BOMB BAY DOOR CONTROL SWITCH.

Description: Manually operated lever.

Location: Bombardier's control stand.

Function: Provide normal extension and retraction of the bomb bay doors.

NOTE

Provision has been made for use of a portable motor for emergency operation of the bomb bay doors. The motor may be engaged with the screw mechanisms in the right-hand catwalk and the power receptacles are located adjacent to the motor engaging chuck. BE SURE THAT EITHER THE LANDING-GEAR POWER TRANSFER SWITCH (aisle stand) OR THE EMERGENCY CIRCUIT SWITCH (battery solenoid shield) IS IN THE "EMERGENCY" POSITION.

CAUTION

Before opening or closing bomb bay doors when the airplane is on the ground, be sure that the area traversed by the doors is clear. This precaution will be taken to prevent possible serious injury to personnel who might be caught in or struck by bomb bay doors.

(h) BOMB SIGNAL SWITCH.

Description: Three-position, toggle switch.

Location: Bombardier's instrument panel.

Function: Allows choice of "BRIGHT," "OFF," and "DIM" operation of the bomb formation lamp.

(8) TURRET CONTROLS.

(a) FOUR CONTROL BOXES.

Description: Switch boxes.

Location: At each gunner's station. One control box serves both side gunners.

Function: Provide control of power and power breakers. Operates the gun, computers, and cameras.

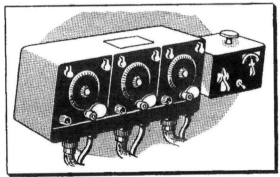

Figure 25—Command Radio Remote Control

(b) SELECTOR SWITCH BOX.

Description: Switch box.

Location: On pedestal of upper gunner's seat.

Function: Allow side gunners to select secondary control.

(9) RADIO CONTROLS.

(a) LIAISON SET.

1. RECEIVER.

Location: Radio operator's table.

Operation: Direct control.

2. TRANSMITTER.

Location: Radio operator's table.

Operation: Direct control. Additional tuning units are stowed under the radio operator's table and in the aft pressurized compartment.

3. TRANSMITTER KEY.

Location: Radio operator's table aft of the liaison receiver.

Operation: To key the transmitter when transmitting "CW" or "TONE."

4. MONITOR SWITCH.

Description: Double-throw, toggle switch.

Location: Radio compass relay shield located under the liaison radio transmitter.

Function: Allow simultaneous operation of the liaison receiver and transmitter for test purposes.

5. ANTENNA TRANSFER SWITCH.

Description: Handle.

Location: Shield above the radio operator's table.

Function: Allows choice of antenna operation, employing either the right-hand wing skin or the trailing antenna.

6. TRAILING ANTENNA REEL CONTROL.

Description: Control box.

Location: Radio operator's table.

Function: Provides control of the reel motor. A red signal lamp will illumine if the landing gear is lowered while the trailing antenna is extended.

7. TRAILING ANTENNA FAIR-LEAD CONTROL.

Description: Lever.

Location: Under the edge of the radio operator's table.

Function: Angularly retracts and extends the antenna fair-lead by means of a cable linkage.

(b) COMMAND RADIO SET.

1. RECEIVERS.

Description: Three receivers are controlled by a remote control box mounted on base of pilot's control stand.

Location: On the cabin side wall above the radio operator's station.

Function: Interplane or air-to-ground communication.

2. TRANSMITTERS.

Description: Two transmitters remotely controlled by a control box mounted on the cabin side wall at the pilot's station.

Location: Cabin side wall above the radio operator's station.

Function: Interplane or air-to-ground communication.

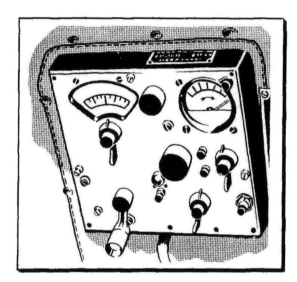

Figure 26—Radio Compass Control Box

(c) RADIO COMPASS.

1. RECEIVER.

Description: A "CW-VOICE" receiver remotely controlled from the control box mounted on the side wall at the copilot's position, or from the control box mounted above the radio operator's table.

Location: Upper left portion of forward bomb bay.

(d) INTERPHONE.

1. AMPLIFIER.

Description: Automatic.

Location: Command radio modulator above radio operator's table.

Function: Amplify intraplane communication. The interphone amplifier has no switch and is in operation whenever the power circuits are energized.

2. JACK BOXES.

Description: Selector switch knob and volume knob.

Location: At each active station in the pressurized cabins.

Function: To allow selective reception or transmission by use of head sets and microphones.

3. MICROPHONE SWITCHES.

Description: Thumb switches.

Location: All interphone stations have cord-type switches except pilots' stations where thumb switches are located on the aileron control wheels, and the fire control where the switch is in the pistol-shaped grip.

Function: Turn microphone off and on.

4. VOICE-RANGE FILTER KNOB.

Description: Knob.

Location: Control boxes on cabin side walls beside pilot and copilot.

Function: Allow selective reception of either the voice or range signals during their simultaneous transmissions.

(e) IFF RADIO (SCR 595 or 695).

Description: Control box.

Location: On the pressure bulkhead at the radio operator's station.

Operation: Airplane identification.

The control box contains selector switches, an "ON-OFF" toggle switch, and an emergency toggle switch. Additional controls, (an "ON-OFF" toggle switch and an emergency switch), protected by a guard, are installed on the top of the pilot's instrument panel.

(f) ARR RADIO (SCR515A).

Description: Control box.

Location: On the top of the pilot's instrument panel.

Operation: Remote Control is accomplished at the pilot's station by means of the control box and the coder switch.

(g) RC-103 RADIO.

Description: Control box.

Location: Oxygen panel at pilot's station.

Function: Lateral guidance during landing operation.

Operation: Provision is made in the control box for monitoring the receiver, switching to one of the six available frequencies, and turning the receiver on and off.

(10) LIGHTING.

(a) IDENTIFICATION LIGHTS.

Description: Push button and four toggles.

Location: Aisle stand.

Function: Identification and signaling.

(b) POSITION LIGHT SWITCHES.

Description: Two, three-position toggle switches.

Location: Aisle stand.

Function: Allows choice of "BRIGHT," "OFF," and "DIM" operation of the position lights.

(c) FORMATION LIGHTS RHEOSTAT.

Description: Knob.

Location: Aisle stand.

Function: Control illumination of the formation lights.

(d) LANDING LIGHT SWITCHES.

Description: Two, three-position toggle switches.

Location: Aisle stand.

Function: Provide control of the retractable landing lights mounted in each wing. The lamps light automatically when extended and may be extended down to 85 degrees.

(e) LANDING-GEAR SPOTLIGHT SWITCH.

Description: Toggle switch.

Location: Engineer's auxiliary switch panel.

Function: Provide control of the wheel well lights employed to illuminate the landing gear, when checking its extended position at night.

(f) FLUORESCENT LIGHTS.

Description: Knobs.

Location: Bombardier's instrument panel, pilot's auxiliary panel, copilot's auxiliary panel, and engineer's auxiliary switch panel.

Function: Start and operate fluorescent lamps.

Operation: A starter-rheostat controls each light and is provided with "OFF," "DIM," "ON," and "START" positions. To operate, turn the knob to the "START" position for approximately 2 seconds. Releasing the knob allows it to snap to the "ON" position. If desired, the knob may then be turned to the "DIM" position to reduce the illumination.

(g) COPILOT'S COMPASS LAMP RHEOSTAT.

Description: Knob.

Location: Copilot's auxiliary panel.

Function: Vary the illumination of the copilot's magnetic compass.

(11) MISCELLANEOUS CONTROLS.

(a) BATTERY SWITCH.

Description: Toggle switch.

Location: Engineer's switch panel.

Function: Disconnect the battery. This switch is wired in series with the master ignition switches, and in order to close the battery circuit the master ignition switches must be "ON."

(b) GENERATOR SWITCHES.

Description: Toggle switches.

Location: Engineer's switch panel.

Function: Provide control of the generators through the reverse current relays.

(c) GENERATOR SELECTOR SWITCH.

Description: Knob.

Location: Engineer's instrument panel.

Function: Allow choice of current and voltage indications for any of the six generators of the main power plant. In addition voltage indication of the auxiliary power unit output may be selected by this switch.

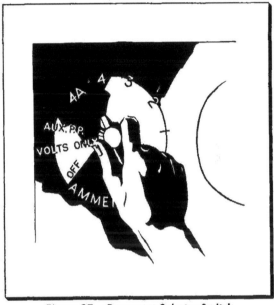

Figure 27—Generator Selector Switch.

(d) INVERTER SELECTOR SWITCH.

Description: Three-position toggle.

Location: Engineer's switch panel.

Function: Allow choice of either of the inverters as a source of a-c power.

(e) EMERGENCY POWER TRANSFER SWITCH.

Description: Two-position toggle.

Location: Battery solenoid shield near the auxiliary power plant.

Function: Transfer the battery and auxiliary power to the emergency power bus for emergency operation of the landing gear, wing flaps, and bomb bay doors.

(f) PITOT HEAT SWITCH.

Description: Toggle switch.

Location: Engineer's switch panel.

Function: Provide control of pitot tube heaters.

(g) SURFACE DE-ICER SWITCH.

Description: Toggle switch.

Location: Engineer's switch panel.

Function: Actuation of this switch closes the air unloading valves and actuates the motor-driven distributor switch, for progressive operation of the de-icer boots.

(h) CAMERA SWITCH.

Description: Toggle switch.

Location: Bombardier's instrument panel.

Function: Provide remote control of photographic equipment.

(i) ALARM BELL SWITCH.

Description: Toggle switch.

Location: Aisle stand.

Function: Permit the pilot to operate warning bells in the aft pressurized cabin and tail gunner's compartment.

4. NIGHT-FLYING PROVISIONS.

a. GENERAL.—The following night-flying provisions have been made for the safety, convenience, and comfort of the flight personnel. In this section no mention will be made of the description, function, and location of the night-flying equipment controls as that information is contained in section I, paragraph 3.

b. EXTERIOR LIGHTING.—Four recognition lights (one each: white, red, green, and amber) are installed in accordance with standard Army Air Force practice. Three position lights are installed; one in the forward edge of each wing tip, and one on the lower aft surface of the tail gunner's compartment. A total of nine blue formation lights are located as follows: two lights on each inboard, one light on each outboard upper wing surface and three lights on the center line of the upper surface of the fuselage. A retractable-type landing light is mounted flush with the lower wing surface on the inboard end of each outboard wing. A portable signal lamp, furnished with interchangeable filters, is stowed in the upper portion of the left-hand side of the fuselage aft of the pilot, and is used for interplane signaling.

c. INTERIOR LIGHTING.—Dome lights are provided as follows: Three in the forward pressurized compartment; two in the aft pressurized compartment; three in the aft unpressurized compartment; and four vapor-proof lights in each of the two bomb bays. Table lights are furnished the bombardier, radio operator, and navigator. An extension light is provided in the aft unpressurized area near the auxiliary power plant. Small adjustable spotlights are furnished for the tail gunner, upper gunner, left-hand gunner, right-hand gunner, radio operator, navigator, pilot, and copilot.

d. MISCELLANEOUS NIGHT-FLYING EQUIPMENT.

(1) NIGHT-FLYING CURTAIN.—A night-flying curtain is provided which may be used to separate the pilot's, copilot's, bombardier's, and engineer's stations from the radio operator's and navigator's stations.

(2) FLARES.—Night flares are furnished for use with the drift recorder during night flights.

SECTION II

OPERATING

INSTRUCTIONS

1. FLIGHT RESTRICTIONS.

a. This airplane must not be flown if the center of gravity is found to be less than 18 percent or more than 32 percent of the mean aerodynamic chord (MAC). If these limits are exceeded, the airplane will be unstable. Consult AN 01-1-40 for instructions in determining the center of gravity.

b. The following maneuvers are prohibited: loop, dive, spin, Immelmann turn, inverted flight, roll, and vertical bank.

c. Observe the air-speed restrictions indicated on placards in the airplane.

2. PILOT'S AND COPILOT'S CHECK LIST.

a. BEFORE STARTING ENGINES.

   (1) Visual inspection of exterior of airplane.

   (2) Crew inspection.

   (3) Combat station inspection.

   (4) Parking brakes "ON," blocks under wheels.

   (5) Emergency landing-gear release.

   (6) Emergency bomb bay door release.

   (7) Emergency cabin air-pressure release.

   (8) Pilot's overcontrol "OFF."

   (9) Alarm bell.

   (10) Engineer's log.

   (11) Parachute.

   (12) Clothing.

   (13) Check oxygen supply pressure.

   (14) Life preserver.

   (15) Lights.

b. DURING WARM-UP.

   (1) Engines.

   (2) Instruments—uncage and check vacuum.

   (3) Radio — check out command set and radio compass.

   (4) Throttle brake—adjust.

c. BEFORE TAKE-OFF.

   (1) Turrets.

   (2) Bomb bay doors "CLOSED."

   (3) Flight controls—unlock and check operation visually.

   (4) Trim tabs "NEUTRAL."

   (5) Hydraulic system—check supply and pressure.

   (6) Vacuum pressure—check.

   (7) A.F.C.E. servo switches "OFF."

   (8) Engine run-up.

   (9) Wing flaps—check operation and set for take-off.

   (10) Engineer.

   (11) Crew.

   (12) Windows and hatches "CLOSED."

d. EMERGENCY TAKE-OFF. — If an emergency take-off is necessary before the engines are completely warmed up, it will be necessary to dilute the oil to lower its viscosity to a point where there will be no danger of the hose connections being blown loose. Check all flight controls. Be sure that the fuel boost pumps are "ON" and the mixture controls are in "AUTOMATIC RICH." Set the turbosupercharger selector to "8" (47.5 inches Hg, military rated power) and propellers at 2600 rpm.

e. ENGINE FAILURE DURING TAKE-OFF.—If an engine fails during take-off, feather the propeller immediately and shut off fuel valve and mixture control. Retract landing gear as soon as possible. Use trim tabs to compensate for unbalanced condition.

f. DURING FLIGHT.

   (1) Landing gear.

   (2) Power.

   (3) Wing flaps.

g. ENGINE FAILURE DURING FLIGHT.

   (1) If engine failure occurs during flight, turn A.F.C.E. master switch "OFF," if it is on; close throttle and cowl flaps, cut-off mixture and shut off booster pump controls for engine affected. Feather the propeller and trim ship to correct any unbalance. A.F.C.E. master switch may then be turned on.

CAUTION

Do not attempt to feather more than one propeller at a time as this uses excessive amounts of current.

   (2) If the engine will not be operated again during flight, transfer the remaining fuel to the other engines, as desired.

h. BEFORE LANDING.

(1) A.F.C.E.

(2) Turrets.

(3) Engineer.

(4) Stall speed.

(5) Flight and engine instruments.

(6) Propellers.

(7) Turbosuperchargers.

(8) Wing flaps.

(9) Gear.

(10) Trim tabs.

(11) Throttle brake.

i. CROSS-WIND LANDING.—Landing under cross-wind and gusty conditions should be less critical for this airplane with its tricycle landing gear than with planes having the conventional type gear. However, as much caution as possible should be exercised in operating the aileron controls, trimming the ship for perfect balance, and heading into the wind. Just prior to the actual landing, the airplane should be turned to head in the direction desired, and brought to a stop as promptly as conditions permit.

j. EMERGENCY TAKE-OFF IF LANDING IS NOT COMPLETED.—If it is necessary to effect a take-off due to an unsatisfactory landing attempt, the following procedure will be noted:

Open throttles wide. Do not exceed 47.5 inches Hg. Turn propeller speed control to "INCREASE RPM." Set at approximately 2600 rpm. *Do not exceed 2880 rpm.*

Raise landing gear. Raise wing flaps to 25 degrees.

k. AFTER LANDING.

(1) Wing flaps "UP."

(2) Turbosupercharger.

(3) Propellers.

(4) Cowl flaps.

(5) Parking brake "ON."

(6) Radio "OFF."

(7) Flight instruments "OFF."

(8) Crew inspection.

3. ENGINEER'S CHECK LIST.

a. BEFORE STARTING ENGINES.

(1) Check Form 1.

(2) Check Form F, weight and balance clearance (AN 01-1-40).

(3) Propellers pulled through by hand.

(4) Emergency flap motor.

(5) Parachutes.

(6) Oxygen.

(7) Clothing.

(8) Life preserver.

(9) Battery switch "ON."

(10) Pilot's emergency switch "ON."

(11) Master switch "ON."

(12) Auxiliary power plant — order started and warmed up.

(13) Lights.

(14) Controls—check for freedom of movement.

(15) Hydraulic system—main and emergency 1000 pounds per square inch. Emergency hydraulic system servicing valve "OFF."

(16) Parking brakes "ON," blocks under wheels.

(17) Cabin pressure release valve.

(18) Fuel quantity—check.

(19) Oil quantity—check.

(20) Inverter switch "ON," test both inverters.

(21) Cowl flaps "OPEN."

(22) Oil cooler shutters.

(23) Intercooler shutters as necessary.

(24) Propellers—low pitch.

(25) Turbosupercharger.

(26) Fuel valves "OPEN."

(27) Mixture controls "IDLE CUT-OFF."

(28) Fuel boosters "ON"—adjust fuel boost pressure.

(29) Fire extinguishers.

(30) Magneto switch.

b. DURING WARM-UP.

(1) Oil pressure—nose.

(2) Oil pressure—rear.

(3) Fuel pressure.

(4) Cylinder head temperature.

(5) Oil temperature.

(6) Wing de-icers.

(7) Generator switches "ON."

(8) Vacuum.

c. BEFORE TAKE-OFF.

(1) Cabin supercharger.

(2) Magneto drop.

(3) Generators.

(4) Cowl flaps.

(5) Fuel booster.

(6) Cylinder head temperature.

(7) Oil pressure—nose.

(8) Oil pressure—rear.

(9) Oil temperature.

d. FIRE IN NACELLE AT ENGINE START.

(1) The following procedure is for fire in a single engine and controls mentioned are for the engine affected. If fire is observed in a nacelle the engineer will immediately do the following:

(2) Move mixture controls to "IDLE CUT-OFF."

(3) Close fuel shut-off valve.

(4) Stop booster pump.

(5) Set fire extinguisher to engine on fire.

(6) Leave cowl flaps "OPEN" to allow ground

crew to attempt to extinguish the fire. If no ground crew is available, or if their attempts are unsuccessful, close cowl flaps and "PULL" fire extinguisher charges as directed by pilot.

(7) Be sure that all used CO_2 bottles are replaced before resuming operations.

e. DURING FLIGHT.

(1) Fuel booster pump.

(2) Auxiliary power plant—order stopped after gear and flap are retracted.

(3) Cowl flaps as required.

(4) Intercooler shutters.

(5) Oil cooler shutters.

(6) Mixture.

(7) Oil pressure—nose.

(8) Oil pressure—rear.

(9) Fuel pressure.

(10) Cylinder head temperature.

(11) Oil temperature.

(12) Cabin supercharger system.

(13) Log.

f. BEFORE LANDING.

(1) Weight and center of gravity.

(2) Auxiliary power plant — order started and warmed up.

(3) Mixture "AUTO-RICH."

(4) Fuel booster pumps "ON."

(5) Oil pressure—nose.

(6) Oil pressure—rear.

(7) Oil temperature.

(8) Cylinder head temperature.

(9) Fuel pressure.

(10) Cabin supercharger system.

(11) De-icers "OFF."

(12) Hydraulic system—check supply and pressure.

(13) Magneto drop.

g. AFTER LANDING.

(1) Cowl flaps "OPEN."

(2) Intercooler shutters.

(3) Oil cooler shutters.

(4) Parking brakes and blocks.

(5) Oil dilution when necessary.

(6) Auxiliary power plant—order that it be shut down.

(7) All switches "OFF."

(8) Throttle and control lock.

4. BOMBARDIER'S CHECK LIST.

a. BEFORE STARTING ENGINES.

(1) Install sight.

(2) Bombardier kit-target information and weather.

(3) Bomb load.

b. DURING WARM-UP.

(1) Free air temperature.

(2) Pressure altitude.

(3) Complete preflight of sight.

c. BEFORE TAKE-OFF.

(1) Interphone and P.D.I.

(2) Clothing, oxygen, and parachute.

d. DURING FLIGHT.

(1) Compute altitude.

(2) Set trail and disc speed.

(3) Set approximate dropping angle.

(4) Observe.

(5) Bomb objective.

e. BEFORE LANDING.

(1) Overnight settings on sight.

(2) Cover sight.

f. AFTER FLIGHT.

(1) Combat station in order.

(2) Report any equipment malfunction.

(3) Prepare reports.

5. NAVIGATOR'S CHECK LIST.

a. DAILY.

(1) Radio time tick.

(2) Sextant correction.

(3) Navigator's kit.

(4) Calibration of instruments.

(5) Astrograph.

(6) Astro compass.

(7) Lighting system.

(8) Drift meter.

b. BEFORE STARTING ENGINES.

(1) Mission data.

(2) Precomputation.

(3) Weather conditions.

(4) Correct time.

(5) Oxygen equipment.

(6) Parachute.

(7) Clothes.

(8) Life preserver.

(9) Interphone.

c. DURING WARM-UP.

(1) Navigation equipment.

(2) Altimeter.

(3) Timepiece synchronization.

(4) Flux-gate compass gyro.

d. BEFORE TAKE-OFF.

(1) Equipment.

(2) Flux-gate compass gyro.

e. DURING FLIGHT.

(1) Continual navigational procedure.

f. BEFORE LANDING.

   (1) Equipment.
   (2) Drift meter shield.
   (3) Flux-gate compass gyro.

g. AFTER LANDING.

   (1) All switches.

6. RADIO OPERATOR'S CHECK LIST.

a. DAILY.

   (1) Antennas.
   (2) Marker beacon.
   (3) Frequency meter.
   (4) Command set.
   (5) Interphone.
   (6) Liaison set.
   (7) Radio compass.
   (8) IFF set.
   (9) Radar.
   (10) Head sets and microphones.
   (11) Charts.
   (12) Codes.
   (13) Lights.

b. BEFORE STARTING ENGINES.

   (1) Charts.
   (2) Codes.
   (3) Blinker light.
   (4) Antennas.
   (5) Head sets and microphones.
   (6) Frequency.

c. DURING WARM-UP.

   (1) Receivers.
   (2) Transmitters.
   (3) Interphone.

d. BEFORE TAKE-OFF.

   (1) IFF.

e. DURING FLIGHT.

   (1) Transmitter (liaison).
   (2) Net report.
   (3) Radio discipline.
   (4) Marker beacon.
   (5) Radio compass.
   (6) Radar.

f. BEFORE LANDING.

   (1) Net report.
   (2) Trailing wire.

g. AFTER LANDING.

   (1) All switches.

7. GUNNER'S CHECK LIST.

a. DAILY.

   (1) Guns.
   (2) C. F. C. system.
   (3) Ammunition containers.
   (4) Ammunition.
   (5) Ammunition belt.
   (6) Turret domes.
   (7) Operation.
   (8) Heaters.
   (9) Harmonization.
   (10) Lights.

b. BEFORE STARTING ENGINES.

   (1) Visual inspection.
   (2) Ammunition quantity.
   (3) Ammunition belt.
   (4) Sight stowage.
   (5) Sighting blisters.
   (6) Turret latches.
   (7) Lamps.
   (8) Fuses.
   (9) Parachute.
   (10) Clothing.
   (11) Oxygen.
   (12) Life preserver.
   (13) Exits.

c. DURING WARM-UP.

   (1) Charge reset.
   (2) Turret stowage.
   (3) Turret domes.
   (4) Sight light.

d. BEFORE TAKE-OFF.

   (1) Taxi and take-off alert.
   (2) Control surfaces.
   (3) Landing gear.
   (4) Flaps.

e. DURING FLIGHT (approaching combat).

   (1) C. F. C. system.
   (2) Selector switch, turrets.
   (3) Selector switch, guns.
   (4) Coordination.
   (5) Firing.

f. BEFORE LANDING.

   (1) Stowage of equipment.
   (2) Landing gear.
   (3) Flaps.

g. AFTER LANDING.

   (1) All switches.

SECTION III
FLIGHT OPERATING DATA

Flight operating data for the B-29 airplane will be published, when available, as a supplement to this Handbook.

SECTION IV

EMERGENCY OPERATING INSTRUCTIONS

1. EMERGENCY EQUIPMENT.

(For diagram showing Emergency Equipment and Exits, see figure 5.)

a. PARACHUTES.—The pilot's, copilot's, engineer's, and navigator's seats accommodate seat or back-type parachutes. It will be necessary for other members of the crew to stow their attachable parachutes so they will be quickly available.

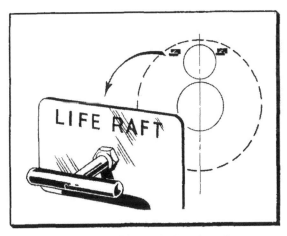

Figure 28—Life Raft Pull Handle

b. LIFE RAFTS.—Two compartments for stowing rafts are mounted on either side of the fuselage just above the wing section. Pull handles, on either side of the forward entrance to the tunnel, will release the doors and CO_2 inflation valve simultaneously. A 25-foot mooring line is attached to the raft and the life raft container by means of swivel snaps.

c. FIRE EXTINGUISHERS. — The following fire extinguishers are provided with each airplane:

One type A-17, or one type 4TB—Inboard side of engineer's control stand.

One type A-17, or one type 4TB—Rear pressure compartment, aft of auxiliary equipment panel.

One type A-2—Adjacent to the aft of rear entrance door.

d. DRIFT SIGNALS. — Twelve drift signals are stowed under the navigator's table and the drift signal chute is in the door just behind the navigator.

e. FIRST-AID KITS.—Five first-aid kits are supplied in the airplane, one each at the following locations: engineer's auxiliary equipment panel, side wall of the engineer's stand, the back of the right-hand side gunner's seat, rear compartment auxiliary panel, and the tail gunner's compartment.

f. HAND AXES.—Of the two hand axes, one is mounted next to the fire extinguisher on the engineer's control stand, and the other is mounted on the rear compartment auxiliary panel.

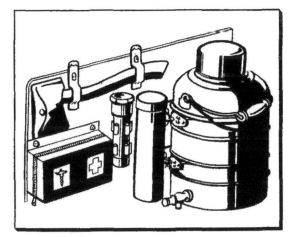

Figure 29—Rear Compartment Auxiliary Equipment Panel

g. FLASHLIGHTS.—Each pressurized compartment is provided with a flashlight located on the engineer's auxiliary panel and the rear compartment auxiliary panel, respectively.

2. EMERGENCY EXITS.

a. The pilot's, engineer, radio operator, navigator, and bombardier exit through the nose wheel well by means of a hatch in the floor beside the engineer's station or

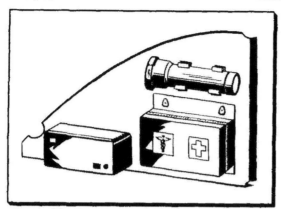

Figure 30—Engineer's Auxiliary Equipment Panel

through the bomb bay. (See figure 2.) On the surface (land or water) the engineer's removable window may be used.

b. The left side, the right side, and the top waist gunners escape through the aft bomb bay.

c. The tail gunner exits through a window at his right.

CAUTION

Any differential in pressure must be equalized with outside pressure before an exit can be made. This is accomplished by pulling the cabin pressure release handle located at the left of the pilot, or on the right side wall of the fuselage at station 646.

3. EMERGENCY OPERATION OF LANDING GEAR.

a. If complete electrical failure has occurred, the auxiliary power plant will be started and warmed up and the "EMERGENCY CIRCUIT SWITCH," on the side of the battery solenoid shield (figure 32), will be placed in "EMERGENCY" position. *This will feed power from the auxiliary power plant into the emergency power bus. The engineer will notify the pilot when the auxiliary power plant is warmed up. (Allow 10 minutes.) Pull the emergency landing-gear release on the pilot's control stand (figure 31) to release the nacelle wheel doors and allow them to fall open. Further pulling actuates the "EMERGENCY LANDING-GEAR SWITCH," beside the pull handle, and lowers successively the nose gear, left landing gear, and right landing gear.*

CAUTION

Be sure to hold the pull handle out as far as it will go, until it is definitely determined that all landing gear is down. Check visually.

b. If the main power system is functioning, but the normal landing-gear motor fuse has blown or a motor has failed, leave the "EMERGENCY CIRCUIT SWITCH" (figure 32) in "NORMAL" position and place the "LANDING-GEAR POWER TRANSFER SWITCH" on the pilot's control stand (figure 11) in "EMERGENCY" position. This connects the main power system to the emergency power bus. Operate the emergency landing-gear release as directed above.

c. The emergency motors may be used to retract the landing gear by holding the emergency gear switch (aft of the release handle) depressed in the "UP" position. No means are provided for emergency retraction of the nacelle doors.

4. EMERGENCY BOMB RELEASE.

a. BOMBARDIER'S RELEASE AND REWIND WHEEL.—A handwheel, to the left of the bombardier's seat, is used for emergency release of bombs and for rewinding the emergency system after release has been accomplished. Two and one-half turns clockwise are necessary to open the doors and release all bombs. The same number of turns in the opposite direction completely rewinds the system.

b. BOMB RELEASE PULL HANDLES.—Two T-type cable pull handles, one on the aft end of the pilot's control stand, and the other at the forward bulkhead in the rear pressurized compartment, on the left side near the communication tunnel, are used for emergency release of all bombs. Approximately 30 inches of travel is necessary to complete the release. The pull handle operates the bomb coordinating unit which transmits the first portion of the pull to the bomb door emergency releases, and subsequent pull to the bomb release levers which drop the bombs unarmed. A safeguard against any bombs being released before the doors are fully opened is provided by an interlock system which locks the release levers until the doors reach their open position.

c. RETRACTION OF BOMB DOORS AFTER EMERGENCY RELEASE.—The emergency release system allows the bomb doors to drop free from the retracting screw. Reengagement of the motor drive is accomplished by rewinding the emergency bomb control mechanism with the bombardier's rewind wheel (2½ turns counterclockwise); then, electrically operating the retracting screw to the fully extended position, where it automatically engages the door mechanism. The doors may then be raised in the usual manner.

5. EMERGENCY POWER TRANSFER SWITCHES.

a. A two-position toggle switch on the battery solenoid shield near the auxiliary power plant transfers the battery and auxiliary power to the emergency power bus for emergency operation of the landing gear, wing flaps, and bomb bay doors.

b. A toggle switch on the pilot's control stand (figure 31) disconnects power from the normal landing gear motors and connects the main power system to the emergency power bus, should it be desired to operate the emergency landing gear, bomb door, or wing flap motors with normal power.

6. EMERGENCY BRAKING SYSTEM.

a. The emergency braking pressure accumulator is charged from the normal system by a valve on the engineer's panel. A pressure gage and a warning light, also on the engineer's panel, indicate the pressure in the sys-

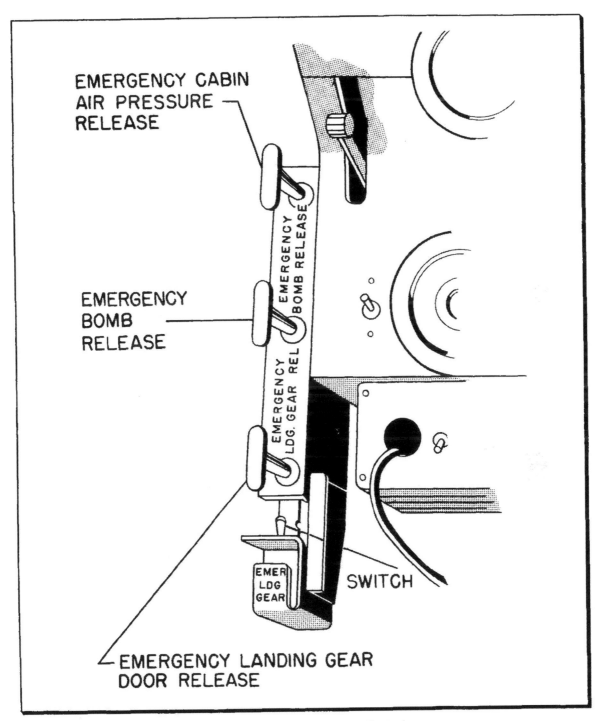

EMERGENCY CABIN
AIR PRESSURE
RELEASE

EMERGENCY
BOMB
RELEASE

EMERGENCY
BOMB RELEASE

EMERGENCY
LDG. GEAR REL

SWITCH

EMER
LDG
GEAR

EMERGENCY LANDING GEAR
DOOR RELEASE

Figure 31—Pilot's Emergency Controls

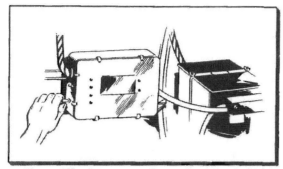

Figure 32—Emergency Power Transfer Switch

tem and visually warn the engineer when the pressure drops below 900 pounds per square inch.

b. A manually operated dual metering valve, located on the aisle stand, is used to apply emergency pressure to the wheel brakes. The control handles provide separate brake operation but are so arranged that they may be operated simultaneously. See figures 59 and 60 for flow diagrams of emergency brake operation.

7. EMERGENCY OPERATION OF WING FLAPS.

In cases of power or motor failure, the wing flaps may be operated by a portable electric motor normally stowed on the upper wing surface of the inboard wing, approximately on the center line of the airplane. The motor is engaged with a torque connection on the top of the midwing section between the bomb bays. The electric receptacle is located adjacent to the torque connection.

CAUTION
To operate the portable motor from the abovementioned receptacle, either the LANDING-GEAR POWER TRANSFER SWITCH (pilot's control stand) or the EMERGENCY CIRCUIT SWITCH (battery solenoid shield) must be in "EMERGENCY" position.

WARNING
Do not lower wing flaps or fly the airplane with wing flaps full down at a speed in excess of 180 miles per hour or with the flaps half down (25 degrees) above 220 miles per hour.

Figure 33—Emergency Brake Levers

8. EMERGENCY CONTROL OF CABIN PRESSURE.

a. If combat conditions are anticipated at high altitudes when the cabin is pressurized, the engineer, upon orders from the pilot, will relieve cabin pressure by means of the cabin pressure relief valve located under the engineer's seat. Lowering of the cabin pressure differential will decrease the possibility of inside pressure rupturing the skin in event of shell fire.

WARNING
Prior to the release of cabin pressure, crew members must be cautioned to wear and adjust their oxygen masks, and if equipped with electrically heated suits to plug them in. Cabin pressure must be released slowly, as a fast pressure drop may cause aeroembolism or "bends."

b. At the lower altitudes where this danger is not present, the cabin pressure may be released very quickly. To permit rapid escape of air from the pressurized cabin and allow the pressure bulkhead doors to be opened in an emergency, pull either of the two cabin pressure release handles. One is located on the pilot's control stand and the other on the right side wall of the rear pressurized compartment near the forward bulkhead.

9. EMERGENCY OXYGEN VALVES.

Reference to figure 53 will show that oxygen is supplied by four groups of cylinders, two serving the for-

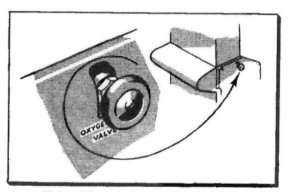

Figure 34—Emergency Oxygen Valve, Engineer's Station

ward compartment and two serving the two rear compartments. The two groups serving the forward system are interconnected by a line incorporating a valve located at the engineer's station. This valve is normally closed but it may be opened in emergencies to make both groups of cylinders available to all forward compartment regulators. The two groups of cylinders serving the rear compartments are similarly interconnected through a valve located in the forward end of the pressurized compartment.

10. EMERGENCY IGNITION CONTROL.

A type C-7 ignition switch located on the pilot's auxiliary panel and two type B-5 switches with linked tog-

Figure 35—Emergency Oxygen Valve, Station 646

gles on the engineer's instrument panel open the battery circuit and ground all magnetos simultaneously in emergencies.

11. EMERGENCY VACUUM SHUT-OFF VALVE.

In the event of a de-icer shoe rupture or vacuum line failure the entire de-icing system and the camera vacuum lines may be shut off by closing the emergency vacuum shut-off valve, mounted on the navigator's filing cabinet. This does not affect proper functioning of the vacuum instruments.

12. ABANDONMENT PROCEDURES.

a. GENERAL.

(1) WARNING SIGNALS.—Three systems enable the pilot to communicate with the crew: the alarm bell system, the phone call system (with their respective switches located on the aisle stand), and the interphone

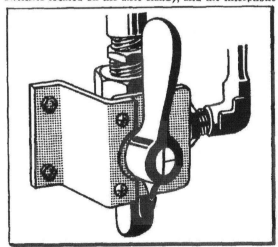

Figure 36—Emergency Vacuum Shut-off Valve

system. For emergency purposes the alarm bell should be operated by the pilot in a prescribed manner thoroughly understood by all crew members. If a commander is aboard, he will direct the pilot to give necessary signals.

(2) EXITS. *(See figure 5.)*—The engineer's, pilot's, and copilot's individual windows and the emergency hatch above the auxiliary power plant will be used for emergency ground exit only, due to danger of being hit by propellers, wing, or horizontal stabilizer. All other indicated exits may be used for abandoning the airplane during flight.

WARNING

Although rapid movement may be necessary in abandoning the airplane, it must be remembered that care is to be exercised to avoid tearing of the parachute. Also, careless rushing may cause body injury to a crew member which would prevent his leaving the airplane.

(3) CREW DUTIES PRIOR TO ABANDONMENT.

(a) All members will fasten parachute and then destroy equipment as designated by Army Air Forces directive. Upon directions from the pilot the bombardier will then release the bombs or auxiliary tanks from both bomb bays and leave the bomb doors open; the navigator will determine the airplane's geographic position; the radio operator will send out the distress signal; and the other crew members will open all doors from which an exit is to be made. The engineer will stand by for further orders from the pilot.

(b) In case of fire inside the fuselage it will be necessary to keep exit doors closed until the order for abandoning the airplane is given by the pilot. The pilot, while giving the above directions and depending upon the circumstances encountered, may wish to use the overcontrol lever and maintain sole control of the airplane. At the proper time he will direct the engineer to close the fuel shut-off valves. When this has been accomplished, the pilot will switch the "EMERGENCY IGNITION SWITCH" to "OFF." If over enemy territory, however, it may be advisable to leave the above switches in operating position, to increase the chances of the airplane burning when it crash lands.

b. CRASH LANDINGS.

(1) GENERAL.—To simplify this discussion the term "crash landing" will be interpreted as meaning any deliberate landing accomplished under emergency conditions, landing gear retracted or extended. It is assumed that no such landing will be attempted unless, in the pilot's judgment, a crash landing is more advisable than parachuting.

(2) DESIGN FEATURES AFFECTING CRASH LANDINGS.

(a) Landing gear, in both its normal and emergency operation, is electrically controlled. (See figure 31.)

(b) The two lower turrets extending below the fuselage will receive the force of the initial impact and may break loose and be forced up into the fuselage on any landing made while the gear is retracted. For this reason crew members are cautioned to take crash stations removed from the lower turrets. This specifically applies to the navigator and radio operator whose normal stations are near the critical areas. If the guns of these turrets are facing aft while making a crash landing the danger will be minimized.

(c) The small propeller-fuselage clearance makes it necessary that inboard engines be completely stopped and propellers feathered prior to a crash landing, to avoid the possibility of a propeller blade being thrown into the forward fuselage compartment. Circumstances will dictate whether outboard engines may be shut down immediately, prior, or considerably in advance of landing.

(d) The fuel shut-off valves should be CLOSED before the engines are shut down. These valves are not of the continuous duty type and require electrical power to position them. Every effort should be made to stop the auxiliary power plant if it is running, as the power generated by it is not disconnected by either the pilot's or engineer's emergency ignition switch or battery switch.

(e) The windows and doors of the pressurized compartments are closely fitted and there may be danger of these windows and doors jamming during very severe crash landings. For this reason it is recommended that prior to landing, the pilot's and copilot's windows, the pressure bulkhead door at station 834, the rear entrance door and rear escape hatch be opened and the engineer's window removed.

(f) No emergency crash stations are provided and it is recommended, as per Army Air Forces instructions, that crew members parachute to safety in event trouble develops. However, if the pilot has only a small crew aboard and decides to risk a crash landing, the bombardier, radio operator, and navigator, after complying with the pilot's orders, will go to the aft pressure compartment and take up crash stations there. The pilot and copilot will remain at their normal stations. Alternate crew members should also take crash stations in the aft pressurized compartment.

(g) Every precaution must be taken to protect crew members from dislodged equipment and to prevent crew members being thrown against the structure. All available parachutes, blankets, mattresses, spare clothing, etc., should be used as padding to protect the crew members and safety belts should be used for additional security.

(3) ACTUAL LANDING.— No attempt will be made to give further instructions upon landing procedure. Every situation is different and calls for a procedure based upon the particular circumstances encountered, and the success or failure of the landing will be directly proportional to the pilot's evaluation of, and his skill in overcoming, the problems involved.

(4) AFTER LANDING.—The airplane has the following emergency equipment:

(a) First-aid kit.

(b) Flashlights.

(c) Water jugs.

(d) Hand axes.

(e) Life rafts.

(f) Fire extinguishers.

(g) Paper cups.

(h) Food locker with Army Air Forces Provisions.

(i) In addition to the above equipment, the individual members of the crew may have other items aboard which will prove invaluable following a crash landing. Matches, extra clothing, bedding, portable transmitter, compass, sheath knife, food, parachute harness to be utilized as a pack harness, automatics and ammunition, cigarettes, signal flares, maps, Very pistol, extra boots, etc., should be considered as valuable aids in meeting the emergency.

c. LANDING ON WATER.

(1) Prior to flights over water the crew should be thoroughly familiar with the duties of each crew member, his assigned crash station, the order and exit by which he leaves the airplane, and the emergency equipment available in the airplane. Several preflight practice drills should be given to acquaint the crew with the problems involved and to reduce to a minimum the time required to complete all preparations and make exit from the plane.

(2) All engines should be operating. Power should be used until a few feet above the water in order to reduce the landing speed and also to more accurately control the time and position of the landing. The propellers will do no damage even if still turning at the time of landing. The direction of landing will depend upon the wind velocity, and the size and shape of waves. If swells are of sufficient width and a slight wind prevails, landing should be made parallel to the crests. However, if the wind velocity is high, the airplane should be landed into the wind to reduce the velocity of the impact.

(3) In making a forced landing on water the matter of first importance is the safe landing and rescue of the crew and every precaution should be taken first to accomplish this successfully. However, many such landings have been made and proved to be not extremely difficult. The next consideration is the possibility of salvaging the airplane.

(4) The empty fuel tanks, including those in the bomb bay, may keep the airplane afloat with some margin, therefore, the airplane might float long enough to be salvaged if such were possible. The life rafts should stay in the vicinity of the airplane, if it remains afloat, since a large object on the surface of the water may readily be spotted from the air.

SECTION V

OPERATIONAL
EQUIPMENT

1. INSTRUMENTS.

a. VACUUM-OPERATED INSTRUMENTS.— Vacuum from the engine-driven pumps operates the turn indicators and flight indicators which are provided for both pilot and copilot. A regulator in the vacuum line maintains between 4 and 6 inches Hg vacuum to the instruments. When the pressure differential between the cabin air and outside air reaches 4 inches Hg, which normally occurs at approximately 13,000 feet, the instruments are automatically isolated from the vacuum system and the cabin differential pressure will continue the operation of the gyros in the instruments.

A suction gage is mounted in the pilot's instrument panel and the de-icer pressure gage is located in the engineer's instrument panel.

b. PITOT-STATIC INSTRUMENTS.—The pitot system supplies impact pressure to the air-speed indicators.

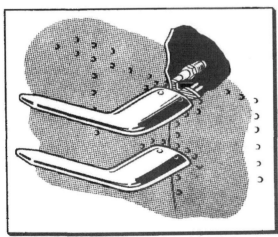

Figure 37—Air-speed Tube Installation

Static pressure to the altimeters, the air-speed indicators and the rate-of-climb indicators is supplied from a static source in the bomb bay. An alternate source of static pressure is provided and may be selected by either the pilot or copilot by means of valves located in their respective panels.

c. ELECTRICALLY OPERATED GYRO INSTRUMENTS.— The turn and bank indicators, provided for both the pilot and copilot, are the only flight instruments which are operated electrically.

d. AUTOSYN INSTRUMENTS.

(1) Pressure lines between the engines and the indicators are eliminated by the use of Autosyn transmitters, located in each nacelle. Autosyn instruments include the manifold-pressure indicators, fuel-pressure indicators, rear oil-pressure indicators, front oil-pressure indicators, and tachometers. All of these instruments are provided at the engineer's station. Duplicate tachometers and manifold-pressure indicators are located in the pilot's instrument panel.

(2) Wing flap indication is also shown on an Autosyn indicator on the copilot's instrument panel. The transmitter is driven by a shaft off the flap mechanism.

(3) Effective on airplane 42-6205 and all thereafter the Autosyn instruments will be changed to the AN direct-pressure type.

e. RATIOMETER INSTRUMENTS.—The indicators for the fuel and oil quantity, and for the position of the intercooler valves, cowl flaps, wing flaps, and landing gear are of the ratiometer type, using direct current.

f. RESISTANCE BULB THERMOMETERS.—Resistance bulb thermometers which measure the resistivity of a special alloy wire and transmit electrically to an indicator, are used for measuring cabin air, outside and oil "IN" temperatures. These indicators are located in the engineer's instrument panel.

g. THERMOCOUPLE INSTRUMENTS.—The cylinder head temperatures are measured by thermocouples at the No. 1 cylinder in the rear bank. Indicators are provided for the engineer and pilot.

h. COMPASSES.— A remote compass transmitter is installed in the left-hand outboard wing, aft of the rear spar, approximately $10\frac{1}{2}$ feet inboard of the wing tip. This location removes the transmitter from the magnetic influence of the armor plate. Indicators are provided in the pilot's, navigator's, and bombardier's instrument panels. The copilot is provided with a standard compass as an optional or alternate means of indication.

Figure 38—Drift Recorder

i. DRIFT RECORDER.— The navigator is provided with a drift recorder for making accurate readings of wind direction and velocity, and for calculating true ground speed. As an alternate provision, drift angles may be observed by means of the tail gunner's gun sight.

2. ARMAMENT.

a. GUNNERY EQUIPMENT.

(1) GENERAL.—Five remotely controlled power-operated gun turrets are provided in this airplane.

(a) UPPER REAR TURRET.

Location .... Station 728.

Armament .... Two .50-calbr machine guns.

Lower limit of fire...... Horizontal.

(b) UPPER FORWARD TURRET.

Location .... Station 177.

Armament .... Two .50-calbr machine guns.

Lower limit of fire...... $2\frac{1}{2}$ degrees below horizontal.

(c) LOWER REAR TURRET.

Location .... Station 945.

Armament .... Two .50-calbr machine guns.

Upper limit of fire...... 5 degrees above horizontal.

(d) LOWER FORWARD TURRET.

Location .... Station 192.

Armament .... Two .50-calbr machine guns.

Upper limit of fire...... 5 degrees above horizontal.

(e) TAIL TURRET.

Location .... Extreme aft portion of the airplane.

Armament .... Two .50 - calbr machine guns and one 20-mm cannon.

Rear limits of fire.... 30 degree angle above and below horizontal center line and 30 degrees right and left of vertical center line. Within these limits a pyramid-shaped area of fire is formed.

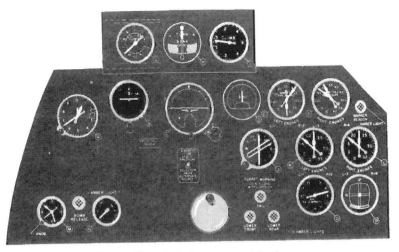

Figure 39—Pilot's Instrument Panel

A—Altimeter
B—Turn Indicator
C—Flight Indicator
D—Pilot Director
E—Manifold Pressure Indicator
F—Manifold Pressure Indicator

G—Air-Speed Indicator
H—Turn and Bank
I—Rate of Climb
J—Compass, Remote Reading
K—Tachometer

L—Tachometer
M—Clock
N—Suction Gage
O—Radio Compass
P—Blind Landing Indicator

NOTE

THE ARRANGEMENT OF INSTRUMENTS
AS INSTALLED IN THE AIRPLANE MAY
NOT BE IDENTICAL WITH THAT SHOWN
HERE.

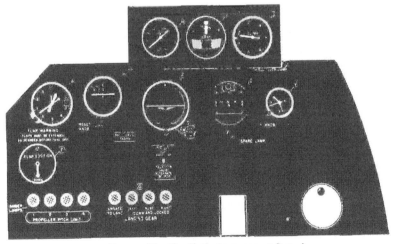

Figure 40—Copilot's Instrument Panel

A—Altimeter
B—Turn Indicator
C—Flight Indicator
D—Compass

E—Clock
F—Flap Position Indicator
G—Landing Wheel Lights

H—Air-Speed Indicator
I—Turn and Bank
J—Rate of Climb

NOTE

THE ARRANGEMENT OF INSTRUMENTS
AS INSTALLED IN THE AIRPLANE MAY
NOT BE IDENTICAL WITH THAT SHOWN
HERE.

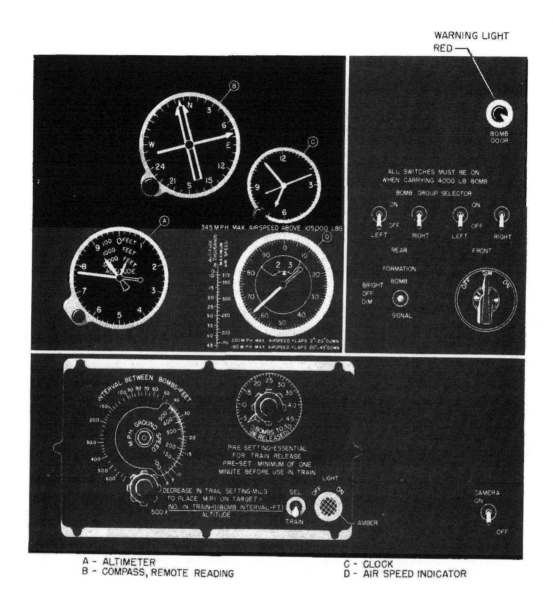

A - ALTIMETER
B - COMPASS, REMOTE READING

C - CLOCK
D - AIR SPEED INDICATOR

Figure 41—Bombardier's Instrument Panel

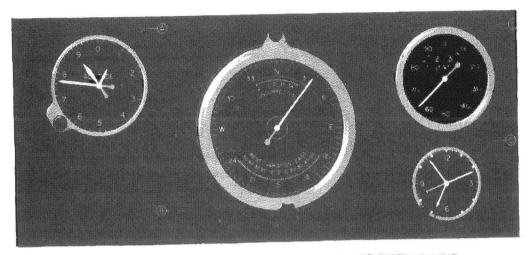

A - ALTIMETER
B - COMPASS,

C - AIR SPEED INDICATOR
D - CLOCK

Figure 42—Navigator's Instrument Panel

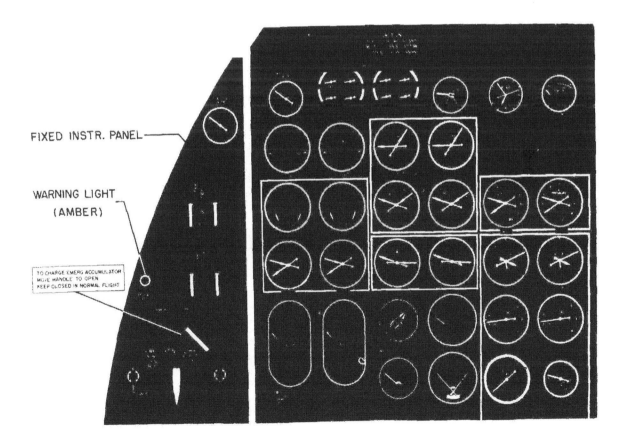

FIXED INSTR. PANEL

WARNING LIGHT
(AMBER)

TO CHARGE EMERG ACCUMULATOR
MOVE HANDLE TO OPEN
KEEP CLOSED IN NORMAL FLIGHT

Figure 43—Engineer's Instrument Panel

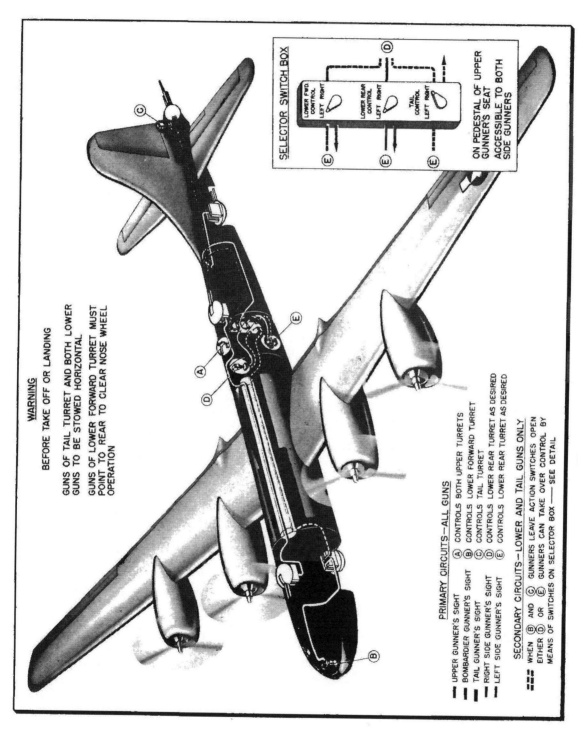

WARNING

BEFORE TAKE OFF OR LANDING

GUNS OF TAIL TURRET AND BOTH LOWER
GUNS TO BE STOWED HORIZONTAL

GUNS OF LOWER FORWARD TURRET MUST
POINT TO REAR TO CLEAR NOSE WHEEL
OPERATION

SELECTOR SWITCH BOX

LOWER FWD.
CONTROL
LEFT RIGHT

LOWER REAR
CONTROL
LEFT RIGHT

TAIL
CONTROL
LEFT RIGHT

ON PEDESTAL OF UPPER
GUNNER'S SEAT
ACCESSIBLE TO BOTH
SIDE GUNNERS

PRIMARY CIRCUITS—ALL GUNS

UPPER GUNNER'S SIGHT   Ⓐ   CONTROLS BOTH UPPER TURRETS
BOMBARDIER GUNNER'S SIGHT   Ⓑ   CONTROLS LOWER FORWARD TURRET
TAIL GUNNER'S SIGHT   Ⓒ   CONTROLS TAIL TURRET
RIGHT SIDE GUNNER'S SIGHT   Ⓓ   CONTROLS LOWER REAR TURRET AS DESIRED
LEFT SIDE GUNNER'S SIGHT   Ⓔ   CONTROLS LOWER REAR TURRET AS DESIRED

SECONDARY CIRCUITS—LOWER AND TAIL GUNS ONLY

WHEN Ⓑ AND Ⓒ GUNNERS LEAVE ACTION SWITCHES OPEN
EITHER Ⓓ OR Ⓔ GUNNERS CAN TAKE OVER CONTROL BY
MEANS OF SWITCHES ON SELECTOR BOX —— SEE DETAIL

Figure 44—Turret Control System

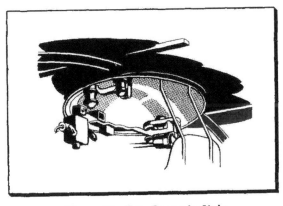

Figure 45—Top Gunner's Sight

NOTE

A 35-mm camera is located in each turret and is shock mounted in such a manner as to permit photographing while firing the guns.

(2) DESCRIPTION.

(a) UPPER TURRETS.—The upper turrets are General Electric No. W8258272. Within the turrets provision has been made for ammunition boxes with a capacity of 500 rounds per gun.

(b) LOWER TURRETS.—The lower turrets are General Electric No. W8258273. Within the turrets provision has been made for ammunition boxes with a capacity of 500 rounds per gun.

(c) TAIL TURRET.—The tail turret is of the airplane manufacturer's design and provision has been made for ammunition boxes with a capacity of 1000 rounds for each of the two .50-calibre guns and 125 rounds for the 20-mm cannon.

(d) SIGHTS.

1. A General Electric-Bell & Howell sight is provided at each of the following stations: bombardier's station, upper gun sighting station, left-hand gunner's station, right-hand gunner's station, and tail gunner's station.

2. These sights control the horizontal and vertical movements of the turrets by means of electrical circuits. When the target is completely enclosed within a reflected circle of light, the guns are in range. The diameter of this circle is varied by adjusting the range finder control.

3. The gunner may position the sight by use of the control knobs on the sights. A thumb controlled trigger is found slightly above each of the two control knobs on each sight, and both guns are fired simulta-

Figure 47—Bombardier's Gun Sight

neously by either one or both of these triggers. An action switch at the left-hand control knob must be kept closed to retain control of the turret being operated.

(e) CONTROL AND SWITCH BOXES.

1. TOP GUNNERS.—Control over either or both of the upper turrets is provided for by a switch box located aft of the gun sight at station 683. Switches contained herein turn on the power and operate the camera, computer, and guns; also, provide the only control of the upper turrets.

2. SIDE GUNNERS.—Through switches provided at their stations, the side gunners have primary control of the lower rear turret and secondary control of the lower front turret and tail turret. Only one sight can be in control of a given turret at any one time.

3. BOMBARDIER.—Primary control of the lower forward turret is afforded the bombardier through

Figure 46—Side Gunner's Sight

the front sighting station. No secondary control of other turrets is possible for this station. When not in use the bombardier's turret sight may be swung to one side of its hinged bracket.

WARNING

GUNS OF THE LOWER FORWARD TURRET MUST BE FACING AFT DURING RAISING OR LOWERING OF THE LANDING GEAR. Warning lights on the pilot's instrument panel illumine if the turrets are not correctly positioned.

4. TAIL GUNNER.— Primary control of the tail turret is afforded at the tail gunner's sighting station but no secondary control of other turrets is possible from this station. Switches allow use of the cannon, machine guns, and camera as desired.

(f) REPLENISHING AMMUNITION.— The upper and lower turrets may be reloaded whenever the airplane is not pressurized, but the tail turret, since it is reloaded from the outside, can only be serviced while on the ground.

(3) OPERATION PROCEDURE.

(a) TRAVERSE.— Both upper and lower turrets have a horizontal traverse of 360 degrees and may be elevated to 90 degrees from horizontal. These turrets are equipped with cam-controlled cut-off switches which protect the airplane from its own fire. The tail turret is equipped with cut-off switches and mechanical stops which limit its vertical and horizontal movement to 30 degrees each side of centered position.

(b) CONTROL OF GUNS.—Control of a turret is accomplished by turning "ON" the turret power switch and slightly rotating the sight to energize the amplidyne generators. The turret is then under the full control of the operator and may be positioned as desired.

(c) SEATING ARRANGEMENT.

1. The bombardier is seated at his regular station.

2. The tail gunner is seated just behind the armor plate pressure bulkhead door at station 1110.

3. The side gunners, one on the left and one on the right side of the airplane, sit facing aft, and have a 180-degree horizontal traverse with a converging angle of vision below the airplane.

4. The top gunner sits on a swivel-type stool, the base of which contains slip rings to convey current from the power lines to the sight. The sight may be moved 60 degrees on the horizontal without swiveling the stool but further traverse of the sight without a corresponding rotation of the stool will break the electrical conduit.

(d) ARMOR PLATE.—Protective armor plate is provided as follows: The pilot and copilot each have a panel behind their seats, and the radio operator and navigator are protected by panels installed on each side of the pressure bulkhead door on the aft side of bulkhead 218. There is a full bulkhead, including door, at

station 706 to protect the two side gunners and upper gunner, and the computer mechanism is protected on the aft, right, and left sides. The tail gunner is protected by an armor bulkhead at station 1144, bulletproof glass on three sides of his head, and armor plate in back of his head. Armor is also installed on three sides of the tail gunner's sighting mechanism.

b. BOMBING EQUIPMENT.

(1) GENERAL.

(a) The two bomb bays are located fore and aft of the wing center station and are separated from the forward and aft main pressurized areas by bulkheads at stations 218 and 646. The bomb doors may be opened at any altitude without affecting the pressurized condition of the airplane; therefore, bombing from extreme altitudes is possible.

(b) Entrance to the bomb bays during flight is through the pressure bulkhead doors to the catwalks, which extend down both sides of each bay. Exit from the pressurized compartments during high altitude flight can be accomplished only by releasing cabin pressure.

(c) The bomb racks, equipped with B-7 and D-6 shackles, are of six sizes for various bomb loading conditions. These racks are attached to the bomb rack supports and the catwalk by means of quick acting pins.

(d) The bombardier opens the bomb doors and releases the bombs by means of controls on his control stand. (See figure 23.)

Figure 48—Bomb Rack Attachment Pin

(2) BOMBARDIER'S CONTROL PANEL.—The bombardier's control panel is located on the side wall at the left of the bombardier's station and provides instruments and controls as follows: altimeter, air-speed indicator, clock, remote reading compass, bomb interval release, bomb formation lamp switch, extension lamp and switch, fluorescent lamp control, camera switch, bomb door indicator light, bomb group selector switches, and the selective-train switch with its indicator light. The bomb interval release may be turned on by placing the selective-train switch in the "SELECTIVE" position; or, if train release is desired, the train release indicator dial (number of bombs) must be displaced from zero.

(3) BOMB DOOR AND RACK CONTROL.

(a) The bombardier is provided with two control levers to control the doors and bomb racks, and an emergency release and rewind wheel is installed for use in event of malfunctioning of the control levers.

(b) The bomb door control lever operates switches which control the bomb door retracting motor and has two positions, "OPEN" and "CLOSED." This lever may be operated independently of the bomb release control, but the bomb release lever is designed so that it cannot be placed in the "SALVO" position without first engaging the bomb door control lever to open the bomb doors. The release lever has three positions as follows:

1. LOCK.—In the bomb "LOCKED" position the bomb racks are locked against any release of bombs except by means of the emergency release levers and wheel.

2. SELECTIVE.—In this position the bomb racks are prepared for single release by manual operation of the bombardier's release switch or by automatic operation through the bomb interval release.

3. SALVO.—In the "SALVO" position the bombs are all released simultaneously and unarmed.

(4) BOMB CONTROL.

(a) Bombs may be released electrically or mechanically. The normal operation is by electric control which provides either automatic or manual control for individual release of the bombs, and release may be accomplished as selective or train bombing. Mechanical control is always salvo, in that bombs are released in emergency by either of the two emergency release levers (pilot's control stand and station 646 bulkhead), or by the bombardier's emergency release and rewind control. These systems are independent of the electrical system and are coordinated by the bomb control unit.

(b) BOMB COORDINATING UNIT. — The bomb control unit is located on the upper surface of the center wing section and coordinates the bomb release systems.

(5) BOMB RACKS.

(a) All bomb racks are of the web-type construction and are interchangeable between bays on the same side of the bomb bay. Eight side racks for the 1000-pound bombs, four side racks for the 1600-, 2000-, and 4000-pound bombs, four center racks for 100- and 300-pound bombs and four center racks for the 500-pound bombs are provided with each airplane.

(b) BOMB LOADING. — To load the bomb racks the bombardier's control lever must be in the "SELECTIVE" position. The type A-2 bomb release units may then be plugged into each active bomb station to be loaded. After attaching the release unit, return the bombardier's control lever to "LOCK" position to prevent possibility of an accidental release.

NOTE

The release units are held into position on the racks by fasteners, as illustrated. To attach the units to the rack the plungers (two per release unit) are pressed by hand into the proper holes on the bomb rack and the small pawls checked. To release, it is only necessary to insert a small diameter rod into the center hole of the clip. This drops the pawls and allows the unit to be removed.

(c) Install the bomb shackles on the bombs and with the aid of the bomb hoisting mechanism proceed to load the stations.

(6) BOMB DOORS.

(a) The two doors in each bomb bay are operated by means of motor-driven retracting screws, two at each end of the bomb bay. Power for this mechanism is furnished through central gear boxes to which the retracting screws attach. Torque is applied to the operating shaft extending between the gear boxes, from electrically driven motor units mounted in the aft right-hand side of the forward bomb bay, and in the forward right-hand side of the rear bomb bay within the catwalks.

(b) The emergency release system opens the doors directly by means of a cable from the bomb control unit to a pulley on the lower end of the bomb door retracting screw. The pulley operates a cam which forces the two followers apart and allows the lower portion of the mechanism to drop free from the screw. Reengagement of the motor drive is accomplished by rewinding the emergency bomb control mechanism with the bombardier's rewind control for resetting, then electrically operating the retracting screw to the fully extended position, where it automatically engages with the terminal at the end of the rod within the screw mechanism. The doors may then be raised in the usual manner.

(c) A mechanical lock, operated by the right-hand door in the forward bomb bay and the left-hand door in the rear bomb bay, prevents use of the bomb release mechanism until the doors are in the "OPEN" position, thus preventing inadvertent release of bombs when the doors are closed. A bomb door safety switch is attached to each bomb door and prevents the use of the electrical bomb release circuit until the doors are fully open.

(d) EMERGENCY RELEASE HANDLES.— The emergency release handles are located as follows: one to the left of the pilot and the other aft of pressure bulkhead 646. One pull on the release handle will open the bomb doors and release the bombs unarmed. The slack cable is rewound by the bombardier's emergency release and rewind control wheel, on the bombardier's control stand.

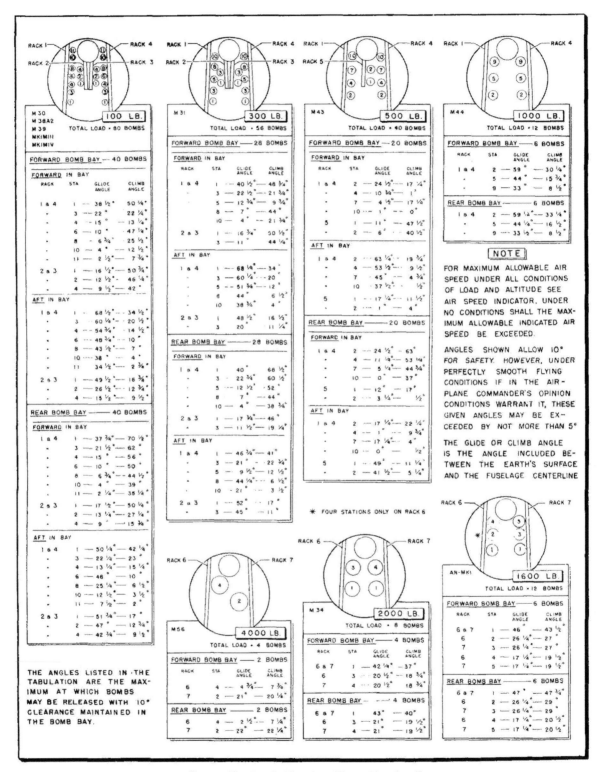

Figure 49—Bomb Fixation Chart (Overload)

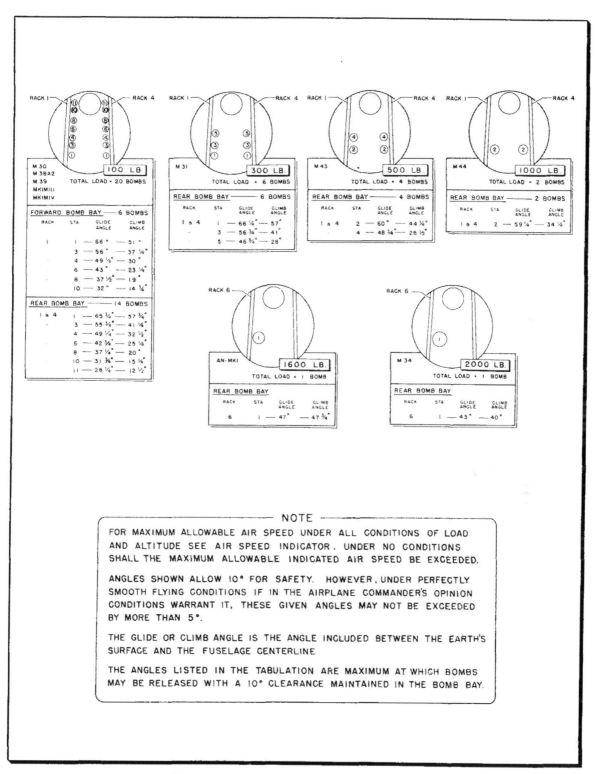

Figure 50—Bomb Fixation Chart (Normal Load)

Figure 51—Release Unit Fastener

3. OXYGEN SYSTEM.

a. GENERAL.—Two separate low-pressure oxygen systems, operating at a maximum pressure of 450 pounds per square inch are provided; one supplying the forward pressurized compartment and the other supplying the rear pressurized compartment and tail gunner. The 12 bottles which supply both systems are the G-1 low-pressure type, and are located under the wing center section between the bomb bays. A two-way check valve is located at the outlet of each cylinder to prevent loss of the complete oxygen supply due to damage of an individual cylinder.

b. FORWARD COMPARTMENT SYSTEM.—The forward system consists of seven cylinders, subdivided into two systems. One of these systems consists of four cylinders supplying oxygen to the navigator, pilot, and bombardier. The remaining three cylinders serve the radio operator, engineer, and copilot. The distribution lines of the forward system are interconnected by a line incorporating a valve, located at the engineer's station. This valve is normally closed.

c. REAR COMPARTMENT SYSTEM. — The rear compartment system, which is subdivided into two systems, is fed by five cylinders, two of which supply the left side sighting station and two relief crew stations. The other three cylinders serve the right side sighting station, the top sighting station, two relief crew stations and the tail gunner's station. The shut-off valve between the two systems is located in the forward end of the aft pressurized compartment. In addition to this valve there is also a shut-off valve, located on the right-hand side wall near the rear pressure bulkhead at station 834, which closes the line to the tail gunner's compartment.

d. REGULATOR PANELS.—Regulator panels are provided at 14 crew stations throughout the ship. Provisions for 2 crew members more than the alternate crew of 12 are made. The equipment mounted on each regulator panel consists of an A-12 demand-type regulator, a K-1 oxygen pressure gage, a warning light, and a type A-3 flow indicator. The panels are located convenient to each crew member's station throughout the airplane. The panel for the upper rear sighting station is mounted on the back of the swivel seat, and the oxygen line is brought up through the center post of the seat assembly and attached to the regulator panel through a swivel joint.

e. PRESSURE WARNING SWITCHES.—Pressure warning switches are located in the navigator's oxygen panel, radio operator's oxygen panel, and the panels at the right and left sighting stations. Each warning switch is located in a separate system and will operate warning lights only for the system in which it is installed. The switches are set to close the circuit and operate the warning lights at 100 pounds per square inch.

f. PORTABLE OXYGEN CYLINDERS. — At each crew station there is a portable oxygen cylinder with a regulator and a recharging hose. These cylinders may be used by the crew while moving about the airplane when it is necessary to use oxygen and may be recharged from the main system as required. The cylinder contains sufficient oxygen to last from 6 to 12 minutes, depending upon the activity of the individual and the system pressure for recharging.

4. HYDRAULIC SYSTEM.

a. GENERAL.—The hydraulic system is used exclusively for brake operation. The system is divided into two units; one for normal use and the other for emergency use. The emergency system is supplied pressure from the normal system, but is isolated by a check valve and a shut-off valve to prevent reverse flow. The emergency shut-off valve is located on the engineer's auxiliary panel. A hand pump is provided on the floor at the left of the copilot's seat for developing pressure when the pump is not in operation.

Figure 52—Typical Oxygen Regulator Panel

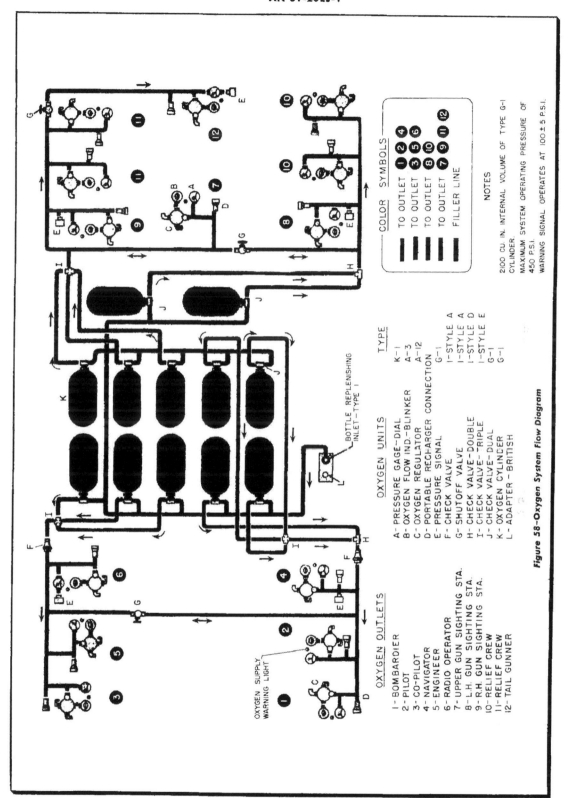

Figure 58-Oxygen System Flow Diagram

OXYGEN UNITS

		TYPE
A-	PRESSURE GAGE–DIAL	K–1
B-	OXYGEN FLOW IND.–BLINKER	A–3
C-	OXYGEN REGULATOR	A–12
D-	PORTABLE RECHARGER CONNECTION	
E-	PRESSURE SIGNAL	G–1
F-	CHECK VALVE	I–STYLE A
G-	SHUTOFF VALVE	I–STYLE A
H-	CHECK VALVE–DOUBLE	I–STYLE D
I-	CHECK VALVE– TRIPLE	I–STYLE E
J-	CHECK VALVE–DUAL	G–1
K-	OXYGEN CYLINDER	G–1
L-	ADAPTER–BRITISH	

OXYGEN OUTLETS

1- BOMBARDIER
2- PILOT
3- CO-PILOT
4- NAVIGATOR
5- ENGINEER
6- RADIO OPERATOR
7- UPPER GUN SIGHTING STA.
8- L.H. GUN SIGHTING STA.
9- R.H. GUN SIGHTING STA.
10- RELIEF CREW
11- RELIEF CREW
12- TAIL GUNNER

BOTTLE REPLENISHING
INLET–TYPE I

OXYGEN SUPPLY
WARNING LIGHT

COLOR SYMBOLS

TO OUTLET ① ② ④
TO OUTLET ③ ⑤ ⑥
TO OUTLET ⑧ ⑩
TO OUTLET ⑦ ⑨ ⑪ ⑫
FILLER LINE

NOTES

2100 CU. IN. INTERNAL VOLUME OF TYPE G-1 CYLINDER.

MAXIMUM SYSTEM OPERATING PRESSURE OF 450 P.S.I.

WARNING SIGNAL OPERATES AT 100 ± 5 P.S.I.

Figure 53—Oxygen System Flow Diagram

OXYGEN CONSUMPTION

NORMAL LOAD CREW

Cubic inches consumed per minute
(corrected to sea level)

Altitude	15,000 Ft.	25,000 Ft.	30,000 Ft.	35,000 Ft.	40,000 Ft.
Pilot	98	177	202	159	128
Copilot—Gun Control Operator	116	208	238	189	153
Navigator—Bombardier Gun Control Operator	116	208	238	189	153
Engineer	98	177	202	159	128
Radio Operator—Gun Control Operator	116	208	238	189	153
Commander—Gun Control Operator	116	208	238	189	153
Total	660 Cu. in. min.	1,186 Cu. in. min.	1,356 Cu. in. min.	1,074 Cu. in. min.	868 Cu. in. min.
Approximate Duration	19.5 hrs.	10.1 hrs.	9.5 hrs.	12.0	14.8

NOTE

The amount of free oxygen (sea level pressure) delivered
by the system between 450 and 50 P.S.I. is 774,460 cu. in.

ALTERNATE LOAD CREW

	15,000	25,000	30,000	35,000	40,000
Bombardier—Gun Control Operator	116	208	238	189	153
Pilot	98	177	202	159	128
Copilot	98	177	202	159	128
Navigator	98	177	202	159	128
Engineer	98	177	202	159	128
Radio Operator	98	177	202	159	128
Relief Crew (Two Men)	196	234	404	318	256
Left Side Gun Control Operator	116	208	238	189	153
Right Side Gun Control Operator	116	208	238	189	153
Commander—Gun Control Operator	116	208	238	189	153
Tail Turret Gun Control Operator	116	208	238	189	153
Total	1,266	2,279	2,604	2,058	1,661
Approximate Duration	10.2 hrs.	5.7 hrs.	4.9 hrs.	6.3 hrs.	7.76 hrs.

Figure 54—Oxygen Consumption Table

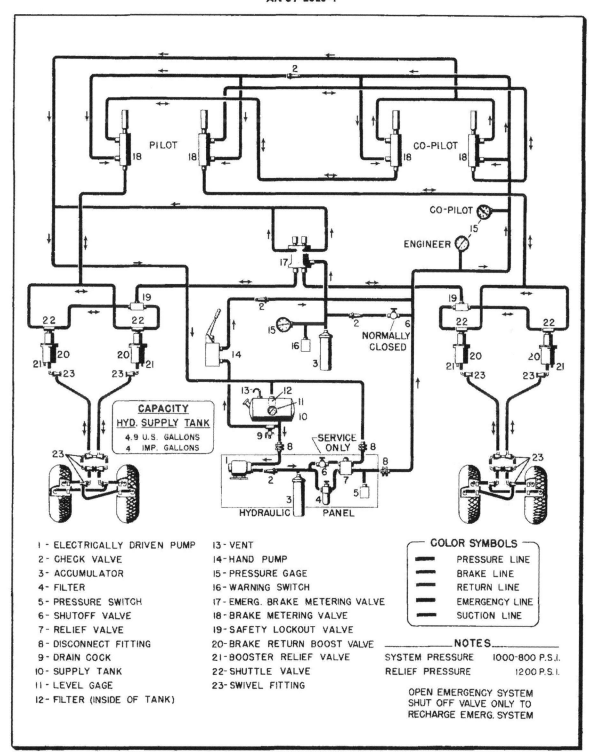

Figure 55—Hydraulic System Flow Diagram

b. NORMAL SYSTEM.

(1) HYDRAULIC PANEL.—A hydraulic panel is located under the floor of the forward compartment near bulkhead 218, containing the following equipment: an electric motor-driven pump, a floating piston-type accumulator, a filter, a pressure switch, a relief valve, and a shut-off valve. This panel is heated by a hot-air outlet from the cabin heating system to prevent the hydraulic fluid from congealing during high altitude flight. The hydraulic pump maintains a system pressure of 800 to 1000 pounds per square inch and is controlled by a pressure switch which closes the circuit and starts the pump when the system pressure drops to 800 pounds per square inch, and opens the circuit when 1000 pounds per square inch pressure is reached.

NOTE

SHOULD THE PRESSURE SWITCH FAIL TO FUNCTION AT 800 POUNDS PER SQUARE INCH THE ENGINEER MAY INCREASE THE PRESSURE BY CLOSING A MOMENTARY CONTACT SWITCH LOCATED ON HIS INSTRUMENT PANEL.

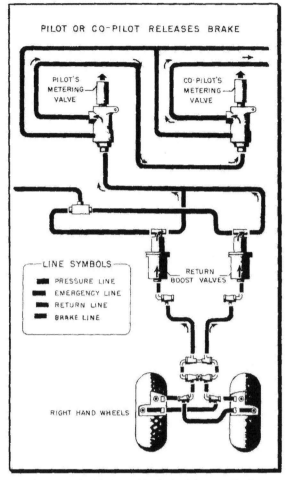

Figure 57—Pilot or Copilot Releases Brakes

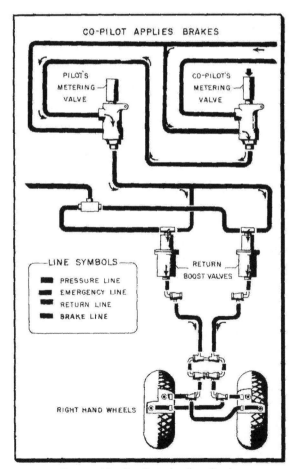

Figure 56—Copilot Applies Brakes

(2) SUPPLY TANK.—The supply tank is located in the forward compartment above the navigator's cabinet at pressure bulkhead 218, and has a capacity of 3 gallons, plus ½ gallon expansion space.

CAUTION

The oil in the tank must be maintained at the proper level, as serious damage to the pump will result should the reservoir run dry.

(3) METERING VALVES.

(*a*) The normal system metering valves are mounted on the pilot's and copilot's rudder pedal stirrup supports, and are controlled individually by toe pressure on either the pilot's or copilot's rudder pedals. In order to eliminate duplicate lines from the copilot's valves to the brakes, the system has been designed so that pressure from the copilot's metering valves passes through the corresponding pilot's metering valves to reach the brakes. (See figure 56.)

(*b*) As the copilot releases his brakes, oil from the wheel passes through the pilot's metering valve before returning to the supply tank.

5. CABIN SUPERCHARGING AND HEATING.

a. CABIN SUPERCHARGING.

(1) Three fuselage compartments are supercharged by means of two engine-driven cabin superchargers, one located in each inboard nacelle, and each supplies air to an independent and separate system of ducts within the airplane. The cabin superchargers are not geared directly to the engines but operate according to supercharging requirements for supplying the two separate systems. Aftercoolers, which control the temperature of the compressed air, are located in the output duct of each cabin supercharger. Cabin pressure is automatically controlled by means of two regulators in the forward end of the rear pressurized compartment.

(2) In climbing from sea level to 30,000 feet, the pressure regulators and cabin superchargers will operate as follows:

(a) From sea level to 8,000 feet the supercharger flow is at a minimum and the regulators allow any excess pressure to escape. This airflow through the cabins thus provides ventilation. At 8,000 feet and continuing to

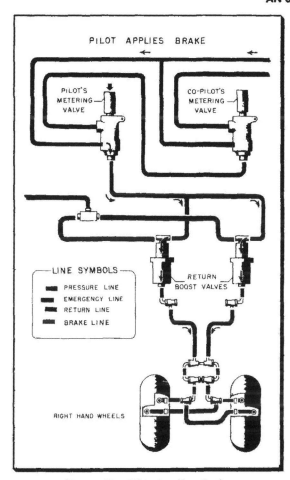

Figure 58—Pilot Applies Brakes

(c) Metering the pilot's valve causes pressure to flow directly from the valve to the brake. (See figure 58.)

(d) Upon releasing the pilot's brake, oil must pass through the pilot's metering valve to the corresponding copilot's metering valve. (See figure 57.)

c. EMERGENCY SYSTEM.

(1) The emergency system consists of an additional accumulator and a hand-operated metering valve located on the aisle stand, and is charged from the normal system by a valve on the engineer's panel. A pressure gage and a warning light, also on the engineer's panel, indicate the pressure in the system, and visually warn the engineer when the pressure drops below 900 pounds per square inch.

(2) A manually operated, dual metering valve located on the aisle stand is used to meter emergency pressure to the wheels. Two control handles provide separate brake operation but are so arranged that they may be operated simultaneously. Metering the emergency valve causes the fluid to flow. (See figure 59.) The return flow, upon release of the handles, is the same as shown in figure 60.

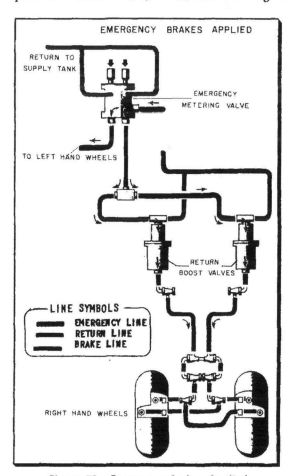

Figure 59—Emergency Brakes Applied

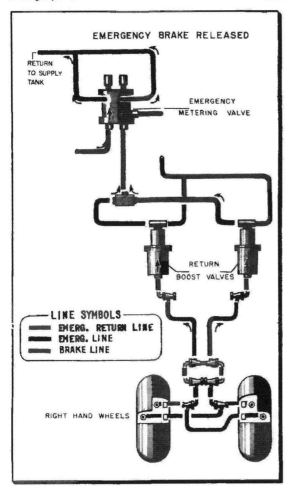

EMERGENCY BRAKE RELEASED

RETURN TO SUPPLY TANK

EMERGENCY METERING VALVE

RETURN
BOOST VALVES

LINE SYMBOLS
EMERG. RETURN LINE
EMERG. LINE
BRAKE LINE

RIGHT HAND WHEELS

Figure 60—Emergency Brakes Released

Figure 62—Cabin Pressure (8000 feet)

30,000 feet, the regulators maintain an 8,000-foot altitude pressure inside the cabin, by allowing only air above that pressure to escape. In the meantime the output of the superchargers increases as the altitude increases.

(b) Continuing above 3,000 feet, the regulators will maintain a 13.34 inches Hg differential in pressure between the cabin and outside air.

(c) Two cabin air check valves are installed in the high-pressure ducts at the inlet to the communication tunnels. Control levers on the engineer's control stand, when placed on "CLOSED" will lock the check valve in the "CLOSED" position and prevent smoke or fumes from entering the cabin.

b. CABIN HEATING.—Heat in the cabin is automatically maintained at 21°C (70°F), or 49°C (120°F) temperature differential, depending upon outside temperature. The sources of heat are two gasoline-operated heaters, one in each supercharging system, and the heat of compression from the cabin superchargers. The heat

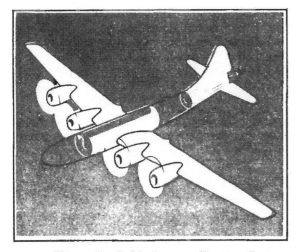

Figure 61—Cabin Pressure (Sea Level)

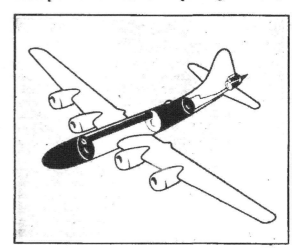

Figure 63—Cabin Pressure (30,000 feet and over)

output from these units is controlled automatically by a thermostat in the engineer's panel. A typical operation of the component parts of the heating system in climbing from sea level to 30,000 feet would be as follows: in the lower altitudes, between sea level and 8,000 feet, the output of the cabin superchargers is at a minimum; therefore, there is little heat of compression. The thermostat, in calling for heat, would first close the aftercooler dampers. If the heat of compression is not enough, the thermostat will start the gasoline-operated heaters. As the altitude increases, the thermostat will call for a decreasing amount of heat from the heaters, due to the increasing heat of compression from the cabin superchargers. As the altitude is further increased, the heat of compression from the superchargers will be sufficient; therefore, the thermostat will shut the heater off and the aftercooler dampers will control the temperature of the air. At extreme altitudes the heat of compression will not be sufficient; therefore, the gasoline-operated heaters will again go into operation. During descent the sequence of operation will be in reverse.

c. EMERGENCY CONTROL OF CABIN PRESSURE.—If combat conditions are anticipated at high altitudes when the cabin is pressurized, the engineer, upon orders from the pilot, will relieve cabin pressure by means of the cabin pressure relief valve located under the engineer's seat. Lowering of the cabin pressure differential will decrease the possibility of inside pressure rupturing the skin, in the event of shell fire.

WARNING

Prior to the release of cabin pressure, crew members must be cautioned to wear and adjust their oxygen masks, and if so equipped, to plug in their electrically heated suits. Cabin pressure must be released slowly, as a fast pressure drop may cause crew discomfort. At the lower altitudes where this danger is not present, the cabin pressure may be released very quickly by pulling either of the two cabin pressure release handles; one of which is located on the pilot's control stand and the other one on the aft side of pressure bulkhead 646.

6. ELECTRICAL EQUIPMENT.

a. D-C POWER.

(1) GENERAL.

(*a*) A nominally 24-volt direct-current, single-wire, ground return system, is utilized for the operation of the major portion of the electrical equipment in this airplane.

(*b*) Six 200-ampere, type P-2 engine-driven generators supply current to the distributing system. The generators are located one each on the inboard engines and two each on the outboard engines. These generators are cooled by forced air and are regulated for both voltage and equal load. An overdrive feature, incorporated into one generator drive on each engine, permits the generator to produce full voltage when the engines are operated at reduced rpm.

(*c*) A type G-1, 34 ampere-hour, 24-volt battery is installed aft of the station 834 bulkhead and is individually vented.

(*d*) Control switches for the battery and each generator are located at the engineer's station.

(2) AUXILIARY SUPPLY.

(*a*) A 200-ampere, gasoline engine-driven, auxiliary power unit is installed aft of the battery. In normal operation this unit supplies power during starting, take-off, and landing. The power unit is started by the START-WARM-UP switch on the unit and may be connected to the power load as soon as its oil gage indicates operating temperature. The auxiliary plant is regulated in a manner similar to the main power generators.

(*b*) The EMERGENCY switch mounted on the battery solenoid shield (near the auxiliary power unit) transfers the battery and auxiliary power to a separate bus system for emergency operation of the bomb doors, wing flaps, and landing gear.

(3) EXTERNAL POWER.—A standard three-prong, external power receptacle is installed in the aft wall of the No. 2 nacelle wheel well.

b. AC POWER.—Two 750 V. A. inverters mounted in navigator's cabinet supply 400-cycle single-phase, 26-volt, alternating current for the Autosyn instruments and 115-volt, single-phase alternating current for the radio compass, the gyro flux gate compass, and the electronic turbosupercharger control. Choice of operation with either of the inverters may be made by a switch on the engineer's switch panel.

c. FUSES.—Seventeen fuse panels throughout the airplane are provided, of which only four, the nacelle solenoid panels, are inaccessible in flight. Six more are inaccessible in supercharged flight: the nose gear solenoid shield, forward and aft bomb door motor solenoid shields, inverter relay shield, battery solenoid shield, and tail skid junction shield. The seven remaining fuse panels are accessible under all conditions: bombardier's fuse panel, aisle stand fuse shield, engineer's forward fuse panel, engineer's aft fuse panel, radio compass junction shield, station 646 fuse shield and turret junction shield. A replacement for each active fuse is mounted inside its fuse shield cover. In the case of the nacelle solenoid panels extra fuses are mounted on the panel side.

d. ELECTRIC MOTORS.

(1) GENERAL.—Control of motor-operated mechanisms, generally in conjunction with position indicators or limit lights, is concentrated chiefly in the engineer's switch panels and the aisle stand. The majority of the motors are of the split field, reversing type with operating limits controlled by limit switches.

(2) FLAP OPERATORS. — The cowl flaps and intercooler flaps are positioned by electrically driven jack screws which are controlled by momentary contact (open-close) switches. The oil cooler flap operators are con-

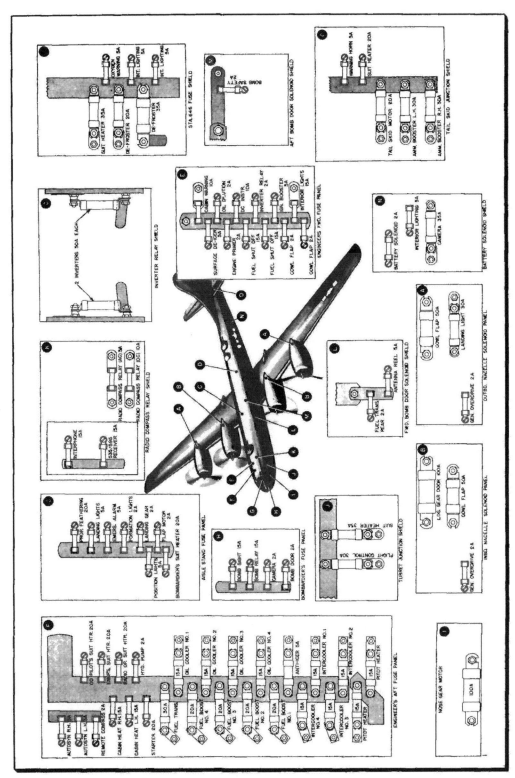

Figure 64—Fuse Location Diagram

Figure 65—Auxiliary Power Plant Details

1. Equalizer Switch
2. Generator Switch
3. Throttle
4. Ignition Switch

trolled by four position switches. Positioning is accomplished by a thermostat (switch in "AUTO") or may be controlled manually by placing the switch in either the "OPEN" or "CLOSE" (momentary contact) position. These switches are all located in the engineer's switch panel.

(3) RETRACTING MOTORS.—The wing flaps and the landing gear, including nacelle doors and tail skid, are controlled by means of up-down switches mounted on the aisle stand. The bomb doors are controlled by switches operated by a lever on the bombardier's control stand.

(4) EMERGENCY RETRACTING SYSTEM.

(a) For emergency operation of the landing gear, (exclusive of the tail skid) duplicate motors and limit switches are provided. They are powered from a separate bus system and controlled through a switch actuated by the emergency nacelle door release, located on the pilot's control stand.

Figure 66—External Power Plug-In Receptacle

(b) The ultimate travel of the cable pull moves the switch to the "DOWN" position. THIS SWITCH IS OF THE MOMENTARY CONTACT TYPE AND MUST BE HELD IN THIS POSITION UNTIL THE LANDING GEAR IS EXTENDED. The landing gear may also be retracted by placing this switch in the "UP" position.

(c) Emergency operation of the wing flaps and bomb door mechanisms is accomplished by means of a portable motor, operating from receptacles located adjacent to the emergency drive mechanisms and connected with the emergency bus system. This motor is arranged to drive through a set of limit switches similar to those of the normal system.

(d) Should it be desired to operate the emergency motors employing power from the normal power system, the power transfer switch, located on the pilot's control stand, should be switched to "EMERGENCY." This switch disconnects the power from the regular system and actuates a solenoid switch to connect the emergency bus system to the normal bus at the aft bomb door motor solenoid shield.

CAUTION

In order to operate the emergency motors, either the POWER TRANSFER switch or the EMERGENCY CIRCUIT switch (battery solenoid shield) must be in the "EMERGENCY" position.

(5) STARTERS.—The engines are provided with combination, inertia-direct cranking starters, each of which is controlled by an accelerate-start switch located in the engineer's switch panel. To operate the starter, the switch should be held in the "ACCELERATE" position until the flywheel has gained sufficient speed, (approximately 15 seconds) then be moved to the "START" position to engage the flywheel and motor with the engine.

(6) FUEL BOOST PUMPS.—The four fuel boost pumps have a constant low speed and a variable high speed and are controlled by ON-OFF switches. The variable speed feature is obtained by means of rheostats tapped across a portion of the pump motor fields. Both rheostats and switches are installed in the engineer's switch panel.

(7) FUEL SHUT-OFF.—ON-OFF switches for the fuel shut-off valves are located in the engineer's switch panel. These valves are positioned in the "OFF" and "ON" positions by separate solenoids, which are not designed for continuous duty. Therefore, a valve position indicator has been devised in the form of moveable plates, bearing dots and actuated by each switch movement, revealing the dots in the direction of actuation. A red dot indicates "valve closed," while "valve open" is shown by a white dot.

(8) FUEL TRANSFER.—The fuel transfer pumps are controlled by a three-pole three-position, reversing switch, installed in the engineer's switch panel. The

switch is labeled "L to R, OFF, and R to L," and operates the pumps through an interlock relay which allows the pumps to run only when both vacuum selector valves are centered in any of their three "ON" positions.

(9) CABIN HEATING SYSTEMS.—Two independent systems are employed to either heat or cool the air, supplied by the cabin superchargers, to maintain a constant cabin temperature of 21°C (70°F). Two thermostats, incorporated in one housing above the engineer's instrument panel, control the amount of heat output by positioning the heater throttles and the aftercooler dampers. These thermostats are of the compensating type, the compensation being derived from the heater and aftercooler controls. This arrangement allows the controls to adjust immediately for the required temperature change, and thus eliminates the time lag (hunting) necessary for a change in heat output at the heater or aftercooler to appear at the thermostat. Each system is controlled separately by a switch in the engineer's auxiliary switch panel.

NOTE

Should a heater overheat it will automatically shut off. To restart the heater, if this has occurred, shut off the heater power supply momentarily by means of the engineer's heating switches.

(10) HYDRAULIC PUMP.—Hydraulic pressure for operating the landing-gear brakes is provided by a motor-driven pump. The system pressure is regulated by a regulator switch operating within the limits of from 800 to 1000 pounds per square inch. For use in emergencies, a switch is provided on the engineer's switch panel, by which means the pump may be made to operate irrespective of the regulator switch.

e. WARNING SIGNALS.

(1) HYDRAULIC PRESSURE.—An amber warning light in the copilot's auxiliary panel is operated by the hydraulic pressure regulator and will illuminate when the main hydraulic system pressure falls below 600 pounds per square inch. Emergency hydraulic system pressures below 900 pounds per square inch are indicated by an amber warning light on the engineer's instrument panel.

(2) OXYGEN PRESSURE.—An amber warning light is located near each oxygen regulator in the airplane. These lights will illuminate when the pressure in the oxygen lines falls below 100 pounds per square inch.

(3) CABIN PRESSURE.—An air pressure switch sounds a warning if the cabin pressure falls below that corresponding to an altitude of 12,000 feet. The warning signal consists of intermittent operation of horns in each pressure compartment. A switch on the engineer's auxiliary switch panel is provided to disconnect this warning, if desired.

(4) LANDING GEAR.—A warning signal, consisting of a steady tone on the horn in the forward cabin, sounds if the throttles are closed while the landing gear is retracted. The warning may be reset as many times as desired. Reset buttons are located aft of the copilot's throttle levers. In addition, a red warning light is located on the copilot's instrument panel. Failure of a landing gear to reach its fully extended position as the throttle is retarded to one quarter position will illuminate the red light. In line with this warning light are three green lights which indicate that all landing gears are in fully extended position.

(5) TRAILING ANTENNA.—The antenna reel control box at the radio operator's station contains an amber warning light and warns the radio operator in event the landing gear is lowered while the trailing antenna is extended.

(6) PHONE CALL.—Amber phone call lights are located adjacent to the interphone jack boxes in both the aft cabin and the tail gunner's compartment. These lights are controlled by a switch on the aisle stand.

(7) ALARM BELL.—A switch on the aisle stand operates warning bells in the aft cabin and tail gunner's compartment.

(8) TURRET LIGHTS.—Three turret lights, mounted on the pilot's instrument panel, are illuminated whenever the lower forward and rear turrets and the tail turret are not stowed in their proper positions. If a landing is attempted while these turrets are not in the proper positions, there is danger of the guns striking the runway in event of a tail down landing, or of the lower forward turret guns interfering with the nose gear wheel doors.

(9) FLAP.—The flap warning throttle switches, located forward of the co-pilot's throttle lever inside of the control stand, are contacted on the take-off, when the throttles are three quarters or more open and the flaps are not down between 20 and 30 degrees. Contact causes the horn in the forward pressurized cabin to blow until corrective flap action silences the warning horn.

f. FIRE CONTROL.

(1) GENERAL.—Three fire control stations in the aft pressurized cabin have primary control of the operation of the rear upper and lower turrets. In addition, fire control stations are provided in the nose and in the tail gunner's compartment for primary control of the forward lower turret and tail turret, respectively. The upper turrets are controlled solely by the aft cabin upper sighting station. However, either the front lower turret (secondary control) or the rear lower turret, but not both, may be controlled along with the tail turret (secondary control) by either one of the side gunner's secondary stations. The three sighting stations in the aft cabin have provisions for defrosting the sighting domes.

(2) GUN SIGHTS.

(a) Gun sights control the movement of the turrets in azimuth and elevation, by pairs of coarse (1:1 ratio) and a fine (31:1 ratio) Selsyns. The Selsyn signals are corrected by single (tail gunner and bombardier) parallax or double parallax (aft cabin stations) computers and are amplified by servo amplifiers. The outputs of the amplifiers are used to control amplidynes (dynamo-electric-amplifiers) which in turn control the turret elevation and azimuth motors.

(b) The gun sights contain firing triggers adjacent to both elevation knobs. Action switches in the gun sight left-hand elevation knobs must be depressed to retain control of the turrets. A rheostat controls the illumination of the reticules.

(c) Gun selector switches at the side and tail gunners' stations allow choice of operation with either the 20-mm cannon or the .50-caliber machine guns, or both. Indicator lights adjacent to each switch indicate which turrets are under secondary control by the gun sight.

(3) CONTROL BOXES. — Switches and circuit breakers for the various power, turret, gun firing, and camera circuits are located in the fire control boxes. These control boxes are located as follows: one at the bombardier's station, one at the tail gunner's station on the left side of the airplane, one at the top gunner's station directly aft of the sighting dome, and one midway between the side gunner's station, accessible to the latter. Associated with the last mentioned control box, a switch box located on the upper gunner's stool pedestal, mounts switches for selecting either of the side sights to operate any of the three guns.

(4) AIR SPEED, AZIMUTH, AND ALTITUDE UNIT.—This unit is located on the cabin side wall aft of the drift recorder, at the navigator's station. By means of this unit the navigator may set barometric altitude, air speed, and temperature corrections for the entire fire control system.

g. BOMB CONTROL.

(1) GENERAL. — Normal bomb release (bomb armed) is accomplished electrically. The electrical release system incorporates controls whereby bombs may be released singly or in train, either automatically in conjunction with the bombsight, or manually by the bomb release switch.

WARNING

When releasing bombs in a glide or climb, the glide angle and climb angle restrictions shown on the bomb fixation charts (figures 49 and 50) must be observed.

Figure 67—Bomb Release Switch

(2) INTERVAL RELEASE.— A bomb interval release unit is employed for train release of bombs. Controls permit variation of the number and interval of bombs in a train release. The unit may be turned on by either setting the selective-train switch in the "SELECTIVE" position or setting the switch in the "TRAIN" position and displacing the "number" index from zero. The illumination of the instrument pilot light may be varied by rotating the jewel.

CAUTION

IN TRAIN RELEASE, THE INTERVAL RELEASE MUST BE PRESENT FOR A MINIMUM OF 1 MINUTE BEFORE RELEASING THE BOMBS.

(3) BOMB RELEASE.—Release units are installed at each active bomb station for the various loading arrangements. The units are wired for release sequence from the bottom to the top of each rack and, in the majority of the loading arrangements, for "layer release" of the racks, provided all group selector switches (4) are closed. In general each bomb group comprises the bomb racks on one side of a bay, and may be withheld from a releasing sequence by opening the selector switch corresponding to the particular bomb group. Rack selector relays automatically select the bomb group sequence and in event of damage or malfunctioning of a group release circuit (open-circuited solenoid or connective wiring), the rack selector relays will eliminate that bomb group from the release train without loss of a release pulse.

(4) SAFETY SWITCHES.— Interlock switches operated by each bomb door prevent electric release of bombs unless the bomb bay doors are fully open. Auxiliary fuel tank safety switches, located on the left side wall of each bomb bay, may be positioned to prevent electrical operation of the release units in their respective bomb bays.

CAUTION

WHENEVER AUXILIARY FUEL TANKS ARE INSTALLED IN A BOMB BAY, THE TANK SAFETY SWITCH IN THAT BAY MUST BE PLACED IN THE "OFF" POSITION. WHEN LOADING BOMBS IN A BAY IN WHICH AUXILIARY TANKS HAVE PREVIOUSLY BEEN INSTALLED, THIS SWITCH SHOULD BE CHECKED TO BE SURE IT IS IN THE "ON" POSITION.

(5) SIGNAL LIGHTS.—While the bomb bay doors are open, a red warning light on the bombardier's instrument panel and a white formation lamp in the tail are illuminated. Bomb release pulses actuate a red filter to change the bomb formation lamp color from white to red and also flash an amber light in the pilot's instrument panel.

h. CAMERA CONTROL.—A receptacle for the camera intervalometer is provided above the bombardier's instrument panel. Also a switch on his instrument panel allows the bombardier to apply power to the camera and camera receptacles located aft of the auxiliary power unit. No provision, however, has been made for remote operation of the camera doors.

i. PROPELLER CONTROL.

(1) PITCH.—An electrical means of adjustment of the propeller governors is provided by reversible electric motors mounted on each engine reduction gear housing. The motor circuits are controlled by four switches on the aisle stand. An amber signal lamp mounted in the copilot's instrument panel will indicate the limit of governor travel in either direction.

(2) FEATHERING.

(a) Propeller feathering is accomplished by means of high-pressure engine oil obtained from motor-driven pumps. Magnetic push buttons installed in the pilot's aisle stand control the pump motors. When operated, the button is held engaged by a solenoid until the oil pressure rises to 400 pounds per square inch. At this pressure feathering should be complete.

(b) Unfeathering requires higher pressures which are obtained by manually holding the push button engaged until the propeller has gained sufficient rpm for the governor to assume control.

CAUTION

DUE TO THE EXCESSIVE CURRENT RE-QUIRED, DO NOT ATTEMPT FEATHER-ING OF MORE THAN ONE PROPELLER AT A TIME EXCEPT IN EMERGENCIES.

j. IGNITION.

(1) MAGNETOS.—Scintilla dual-type magnetos are installed, one for each engine, and are individually controlled by switches at the engineer's station. For emergency use, master switches are provided at the pilot's and engineer's stations which open the battery circuit and ground all magnetos.

CAUTION

MAGNETO GROUNDING PLUGS MUST BE KEPT CONNECTED. REMOVAL OF A PLUG WILL ISOLATE THE MAGNETO IN AN OPERABLE CONDITION INDEPEND-ENT OF CONTROL BY THE SWITCHES.

(2) BOOSTERS.—Ignition booster coils mounted in each nacelle supplement the magnetos in engine starting. Control switches are mounted in the engineer's switch panel.

k. PRIMING AND OIL DILUTION VALVES.

(1) PRIMING VALVES.—Solenoid valves, located on each engine starter, are operated by switches on the engineer's switch panel.

(2) OIL DILUTION VALVES.—Oil dilution valves are connected to supply fuel to the engine oil system lowering the viscosity to permit the engine to start more easily in cold weather. The oil should be diluted for not more than four minutes prior to engine shut-down,

if cold starting conditions are anticipated. These valves are operated by switches in the engineer's switch panel.

l. INSTRUMENTS.

(1) GENERAL.— The electrical instruments in this airplane are used chiefly for remote indication and may be classified according to their power supply.

(2) A-C INSTRUMENTS.

(a) AUTOSYN INSTRUMENTS.

1. Autosyn instruments are essentially means of reproducing, at an "indicator," motion introduced in the "transmitter" by a pressure, temperature, or otherwise sensitive mechanism at a remote location. Each instrument pair (transmitter and indicator) employs a primary or "rotor," energized by 400-cycle, 26-volt alternating current; and interconnected secondaries or "stators" by which the transmitter rotor motion or position, is translated into a combination of currents of varying magnitude, and retranslated into indicator rotor motion or position.

2. Four Autosyn indicators are provided for each engine; fuel pressure, oil pressure, manifold pressure and engine rpm. The transmitters are installed on vibration damped mountings and are connected with dual-type indicators in the engineer's instrument panel. The dual manifold pressure and engine rpm indicators are also provided in the pilot's instrument panel.

3. Autosyn instruments for the left-hand engines are fused separately from those for the right-hand engines.

4. An alternating-current voltmeter, mounted in the engineer's instrument panel, indicates Autosyn primary voltage. This voltage should be approximately 26 volts.

NOTE

Since this voltmeter is connected to the left-hand engine instruments only, a voltage indication will not necessarily indicate fuse continuity for the right-hand engine instrument.

(b) GYRO-FLUXGATE COMPASS.

1. A remote indicating magnetic compass system is employed in this airplane to provide a directive system as free as possible from the influence of motors, armor plate and other distorting factors of the earth's magnetic field. In addition the nature of the "flux-gate" sensitive element, consisting of a set of fixed coils, is inherently free from swirl and acceleration errors. Also, by mounting the flux-gate on a stabilized, electrically driven gyroscope, northward turning errors, caused by the influence of the vertical component of the earth's field while the airplane is banking, are eliminated.

2. The essential components of the system consist of the flux-gate transmitter, an electronic amplifier, and a master indicator. The flux-gate transmitter is mounted in the left-hand wing tip.

3. The amplifier and master indicator are both installed at the navigator's station.

4. The sensitivity of the amplifier may be varied by a knob on the amplifier base. By this means it is possible to compensate for the loss of sensitivity in standard compasses, due to decreasing intensity of the horizontal component of the earth field, encountered in extreme northern and southern latitudes. In normal operation this knob should be set just below the point where noticeable oscillation of the indicator pointer occurs.

5. The master indicator contains a compensating cam which may be set to correct for magnetic distortion, if present at the flux-gate transmitter. A knob on the instrument permits the navigator to insert the magnetic variation prevailing at the airplane's geographic location. The pointer will then read the airplane's magnetic heading directly. A "magnesyn" transmitter (similar to an Autosyn) coupled to the pointer is connected with indicators, in the pilot's and bombardier's instrument boards, which will show bearings identical to that of master indicator.

(3) D-C INSTRUMENTS.

(a) The direct-current class of instruments contains two general types, position instruments and temperature instruments, exclusive of the turn and bank indicators which also are electrically driven.

(b) POSITION INSTRUMENTS.

1. These instruments are employed for remote indication in applications similar to the Autosyns, but where a lesser degree of precision may be tolerated. The instruments employ an electrical bridge circuit wherein a potentiometer (transmitter) forms two variable bridge circuit arms and a ratiometer (indicator) completes the circuit. By indicating the degree of circuit unbalance, the ratiometer indicates the transmitter (potentiometer tap) position.

2. The cowl flap, the intercooler flap, the landing gear and wing flap position indicators, and the fuel and oil quantity indicators are all of this type. Except for the landing gear and wing flap indicator, which is mounted in the copilot's instrument panel, these instruments are mounted in the engineer's instrument panel.

(c) TEMPERATURE INSTRUMENTS.—Indications are provided at the engineer's station for oil inlet, cabin air, and free air temperatures, employing resistance bulbs as the sensitive elements.

(4) SELF - GENERATING INSTRUMENTS.— Two dual cylinder head temperature indicators, installed in the engineer's instrument panel, are connected with spark plug gasket thermocouples. These thermocouples are mounted one on the No. 1 cylinder of the rear bank of each engine, and develop a current proportional to the temperature of the cylinders upon which they are mounted. The current is then indicated by a sensitive micrometer movement calibrated in cylinder temperature.

m. DE-ICING SYSTEM.

(1) SURFACE DE-ICERS.

(a) Ice is eliminated from the wings and empennage by inflation and deflation of conventional de-icer boots. Inflation and deflation of the boots is controlled by solenoid valve assemblies. Each assembly consists of two solenoid valves having common pressure, vacuum and vent ports, and operating alternate tubes in a de-icer boot. These valves admit pressure air to the boot while their solenoids are energized. On release of the solenoid the valve discharges air through the vent until the pressure approaches atmospheric, whereupon the valve transfers the boot connection to the vacuum system, assuring deflation until the next cycle of operation.

(b) Wing de-icer operating sequence is symmetrical about the center line of the fuselage, in order to minimize rolling which would result from asymmetric deformation of the wing airfoil. This sequence is obtained by means of an electrically driven timer consisting of a rotating contactor which passes over the solenoid valve contacts in order. While the timer is not in operation solenoid valves relieve the pressure air overboard.

(c) Operation of the de-icers is controlled by the SURFACE DE-ICER switch in the engineer's switch panel.

CAUTION

DO NOT OPERATE DE-ICER DURING LANDING OR TAKE-OFF.

(2) PROPELLER ANTI-ICER.—Propeller icing is prevented by an anti-icing solution pumped to the propeller slinger rings by two electrically driven pumps, located below the aft cabin floor. The inboard and outboard propellers are supplied by separate pumps, the speed of which may be varied by adjusting rheostats mounted near the base of the engineer's control stand. A switch adjacent to the surface de-icer switch controls both pumps.

(3) PITOT HEATERS.—The heater circuits of the pitot tubes are controlled by the PITOT switch, adjacent to the de-icer switch in the engineer's switch panel.

(4) SUIT HEATERS.—Suit heater outlets and controls are provided at each active crew station.

n. INTERIOR LIGHTING.

(1) INSTRUMENT LIGHTING.

(a) FLUORESCENT LAMPS.

1. The instrument lighting has been specially adapted for night-flying through the use of self-luminous scales and indices, which also fluoresce under the influence of ultraviolet light. Ultraviolet light is projected upon the bombardier's, pilot's, copilot's, and engineer's instrument panels by fluorescent lamps equipped with filters, to vary or exclude the accompanying visible radiation. This filter is attached to an adjustable collar on the front of the lamp.

2. The lamps are controlled by rheostats mounted on the bombardier's instrument panel and on the pilot's, copilot's, and engineer's auxiliary panels. To start the lamps, move the rheostat knob to the "START" position. As soon as the lamp starts, the intensity of illumination may be varied as desired, by placing the control from "ON" to the "DIM" position.

(b) INDIVIDUAL LIGHTING.—The copilot's compass is illuminated by means of a small lamp contained within the instrument. The illumination is controlled by a rheostat in the copilot's auxiliary instrument panel.

(c) SPOTLIGHTS.—Adjustable spotlights at the pilot's, copilot's, navigator's, radio operator's, top gunner's, left gunner's, right gunner's, and tail gunner's stations provide optional instrument illumination. These lamps have self-contained rheostats to vary their illumination.

(d) TABLE LIGHTS. — Additional lights are provided the bombardier, navigator, and radio operator to illuminate their tables.

(e) EXTENSION LAMPS.—A lamp assembly with six feet of cord on a self-winding reel and an on-off switch is provided at station 900 for use when operating the auxiliary power unit or cameras.

(2) DOME LIGHTS.—Dome lights are installed trhoughout the airplane for general illumination, vapor-proof lights being installed in the bomb bays. Dome lights in the unpressurized tail section are operated by either a switch accessible to the tail gunner, or a switch near the rear entrance door. A dome light on the aft face of the aft cabin rear bulkhead is operated from either side of the cabin bulkhead. The three dome lights located in the forward pressurized cabin are controlled by "ON-OFF" toggle switches built integral with the lights.

o. EXTERIOR LIGHTS.

(1) RECOGNITION LIGHTS. — A white recognition lamp is located on the center line of the fuselage upper surface. Three recognition lamps, red, green, and amber are located along the center line of the fuselage lower surface. These lamps may be set for any of several combinations by means of individual KEY-OFF-STEADY switches in the aisle stand. Lights positioned to "KEY" may be keyed simultaneously by a push-button "key" switch installed adjacent to the recognition light switches.

(2) POSITION LIGHTS.— The wing tip position (red and green) lights are controlled by a switch and fixed resistor in the aisle stand. The switch allows choice of "BRIGHT," "OFF," and "DIM" operation of the lights. A similar control provision is made for the tail (white) light.

(3) FORMATION LIGHTS.— Nine formation (blue) lamps are provided; three in the upper surface of the fuselage, and three in the upper surface of each wing, aft of the rear spar. A rheostat with an "OFF" position is provided in the aisle stand to control the illumination.

p. INTERAIRCRAFT SIGNAL LAMP.— A receptacle for supplying power to an interaircraft signal lamp is installed in the rear of the aisle stand. This lamp is controlled by a trigger switch, integral with the lamp.

q. LANDING LIGHTS.— An electrically operated retractable landing light is mounted in the lower surface of each outboard wing. Each lamp lights automatically when extended and is controlled by a switch in the aisle stand.

r. WHEEL WELL SPOTLIGHTS.— Small lamps are provided to illuminate the landing gear at night, when in the extended position. The lights are controlled by a switch on the engineer's auxiliary switch panel.

7. COMMUNICATION EQUIPMENT.

a. GENERAL.—The communication equipment in this airplane comprises radio and interphone equipment arranged to provide communication with ground stations and other airplanes, intraplane communication among the crew members, and reception of range and marker beacon signals. In addition, specialized equipment is provided for automatic radio direction finding and recognition and identification of friendly aircraft. Since the operation of this equipment is of a specialized nature, detailed instructions for its operation will not be given here. Personnel unfamiliar with this equipment should not attempt its operation until a study of the appropriate instruction book has been made. These books are stowed in the forward cabin. The airplane's radio call numbers are located on the pilot's and copilot's instrument boards, command radio set mounting, and on each side of the vertical stabilizer.

b. LIAISON RADIO SET.

(1) TRANSMITTER.

(a) The liaison transmitter is mounted on the forward cabin right-hand side wall adjacent to the radio operator's table and is normally used for communication with ground stations. The liaison transmitter has a frequency range of 200 to 500 kilocycles and 1500 to 12,500 kilocycles which is covered by seven interchangeable tuning units. These units are stowed, two beneath the radio operator's table, and the remaining four aft of the left side gunner's armor plate.

CAUTION
Transmitter operation at cabin altitudes above 15,000 feet is subject to flash-over with some tuning units.

(b) A chart indicating the dial settings for the desired frequencies is mounted on the front of each tuning unit. The calibration of the dial settings is close; however, it is possible to tune the transmitter to the exact frequency of an incoming signal in the receiver by means of a monitor switch located in the radio compass relay shield. With this switch in the "MONITOR" position the transmitter sidetone is cut off and the receiver may be turned on and adjusted to receive the desired frequency. The transmitter key adjacent to the liaison receiver is depressed and the transmitter oscillator dial adjusted to "zero beat" with the incoming signal. The transmitter is then adjusted for maximum output and rechecked in the receiver.

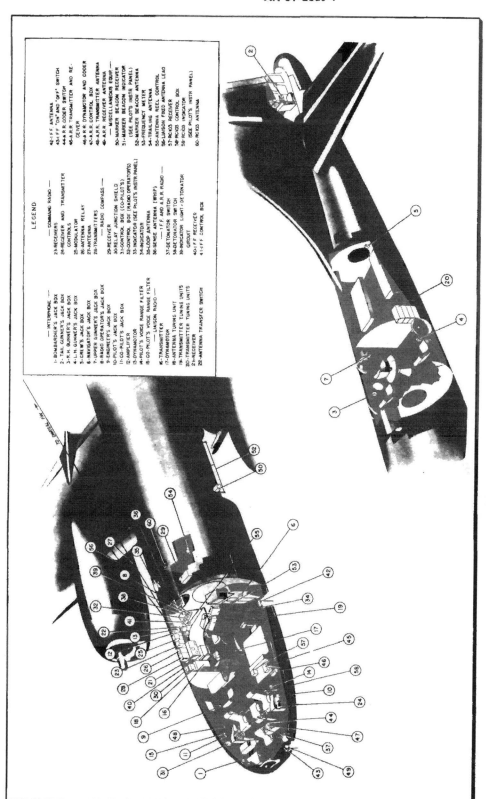

LEGEND

— INTERPHONE —
1-BOMBARDIER'S JACK BOX
2-TAIL GUNNER'S JACK BOX
3-R.H. GUNNER'S JACK BOX
4-L.H. GUNNER'S JACK BOX
5-CREW'S JACK BOX
6-NAVIGATOR'S JACK BOX
7-UPPER GUNNER'S JACK BOX
8-RADIO OPERATOR'S JACK BOX
9-ENGINEER'S JACK BOX
10-PILOT'S JACK BOX
11-CO-PILOT'S JACK BOX
12-AMPLIFIER
13-DYNAMOTOR
14-PILOT'S VOICE RANGE FILTER
15-CO-PILOT'S VOICE RANGE FILTER

— LIAISON RADIO —
16-TRANSMITTER
17-DYNAMOTOR
18-ANTENNA TUNING UNIT
19-TRANSMITTER TUNING UNITS
20-TRANSMITTER TUNING UNITS
21-RECEIVER
22-ANTENNA TRANSFER SWITCH

— COMMAND RADIO —
23-RECEIVERS
24-RECEIVER AND TRANSMITTER CONTROLS
25-MODULATOR
26-ANTENNA RELAY
27-ANTENNA
28-TRANSMITTERS

— RADIO COMPASS —
29-RECEIVER
30-RELAY JUNCTION SHIELD
31-CONTROL BOX (CO-PILOT'S)
32-CONTROL BOX (RADIO OPERATOR'S)
33-INDICATOR (SEE PILOT'S INSTR PANEL)
34-INDICATOR
35-LOOP ANTENNA
36-SENSE ANTENNA (WHIP)
37-DETONATOR SWITCH
38-DETONATOR SWITCH
39-INDICATOR LIGHT - DETONATOR CIRCUIT
40-I.F.F. RECEIVER
41-I.F.F. CONTROL BOX
42-I.F.F. ANTENNA
43-I.F.F "ON AND OFF" SWITCH
44-A.R.R. CODER SWITCH
45-A.R.R. TRANSMITTER AND RECEIVER
46-A.R.R. DYNAMOTOR AND CODER
47-A.R.R. CONTROL BOX
48-A.R.R. TRANSMITTER ANTENNA
49-A.R.R. RECEIVER ANTENNA
— MISCELLANEOUS EQUIP —
50-MARKER BEACON RECEIVER
51-MARKER BEACON INDICATOR (SEE PILOT'S INSTR PANEL)
52-MARKER BEACON ANTENNA
53-FREQUENCY METER
54-TRAILING ANTENNA
55-ANTENNA REEL CONTROL
56-LIAISON FIXED ANTENNA LEAD
57-RCKS RECEIVER
58-RCKS CONTROL BOX
59-RCKS INDICATOR (SEE PILOT'S INSTR PANEL)
60-RCKS ANTENNA

Figure 68—Communications Equipment Diagram

(c) A similar procedure is followed when adjusting the transmitter frequency and checking with the frequency meter (SCR 211). The frequency meter is stowed aft of the engineer's control stand.

(d) When the monitor switch is in the "NORMAL" position the receiver will be silenced while the transmitter is in operation, and the transmitter sidetone signal will be present in the interphones.

(e) The transmitter may be modulated by either the pilot's, copilot's, or radio operator's microphone.

IMPORTANT

When the transmitter is operating, the filament voltage meter must read 10 volts (calibration mark on meter). The RF and modulator filament voltages are checked separately by a switch adjacent to the transmitter "ON-OFF" switch on the transmitter face.

(2) RECEIVER.— The receiver controls are mounted on its face. The "OFF-MVC-AVC" switch turns on the receiver and in addition allows choice of manual (MVC) or automatic (AVC) gain control. Tuning is best accomplished with manual gain control. After the signal has been tuned the switch may be positioned for automatic gain control, if desired. Reception of "CW" signals should not be attempted with automatic gain control. Frequency band selection is accomplished by means of the band switch. Operation of this switch also changes the tuning dial calibration to correspond with the selected band frequencies.

(3) ANTENNA TUNING UNIT.— In order to provide efficient antenna loading, an antenna tuning unit is installed above the liaison transmitter.

(4) ANTENNAS.

(a) This radio set employs both a fixed and trailing antenna installation. Either antenna may be selected by means of the shielded antenna transfer switch, mounted on the cabin bulkhead above the radio operator's table.

(b) The fixed antenna installation utilizes the right-hand wing skin as a radiator. The antenna lead connection is made near the top of the No. 3 nacelle.

(c) The trailing antenna is 250 feet long and is wound on a motor-driven reel through an insulated fairlead, which may be extended angularly by a lever on the leg of the radio operator's table. The reel and fair-lead are mounted in the aft portion of the forward bomb bay on the right-hand catwalk.

(5) TRAILING ANTENNA CONTROL.— The antenna reel motor control box is mounted on the cabin bulkhead above the radio operator's table. The control box contains an "IN-OFF-OUT" switch, a cable operated counter indicating the amount of antenna paid out, and an amber light to warn the radio operator if the landing gear should be extended while the antenna is not retracted. A small knob is provided to set the zero of the antenna counter dial.

DANGER

Do not make any adjustments within the command or liaison transmitters while the high voltage supply is "ON."

Do not remove or replace tubes in any of the radio equipment while the power supply is "ON." Do not remove the covers from or replace fuses in any of the dynamotors while they are running.

c. COMMAND RADIO SET (SCR 274N).

(1) GENERAL.—The command radio consists of two transmitters, three receivers, and auxiliary equipment. These are of short range and are primarily used for airplane-to-airplane communication on the following channels: the transmitting frequency ranges are from 4000 to 5300 kilocycles and from 7000 to 9100 kilocycles; the three receivers have ranges of 190 to 550 kilocycles, 3000 to 6000 kilocycles, and 6000 to 9100 kilocycles, respectively.

(2) TRANSMITTERS.

(a) The two transmitters are mounted together on a rack above the radio operator's table and are controlled by a control box mounted on the cabin side wall, at the pilot's station.

(b) Each transmitter is supplied with a special frequency-checking circuit and a plug-in crystal is used for checking the transmitter frequency only and does not control the transmitter frequency.

(c) The transmitter control box contains TRANSMITTER POWER, TRANSMITTER SELECTOR, and TONE-CW-VOICE switches.

(d) The transmitter selector switch allows a choice of operation with either transmitter. With the emission selector switch in the "CW" position, the transmitted signal will be unmodulated. In the "TONE" position the signal is almost 100 percent modulated by a 1000-cycle note. The "VOICE" position allows the microphone of any interphone jack box (switched to the "COMMAND" position) to modulate the transmitter. For long-range communication through interference, the most effective operation is CW with TONE and VOICE following in that order.

(e) In both the "CW" and "TONE" position the transmitter is keyed by a built-in key located on the top of the control box.

NOTE

Inasmuch as the transmitter dynamotor operates continuously while the selector is in the "TONE" or "CW" position, the selector should be left in "VOICE" to reduce power drain and promote dynamotor life, unless continued Tone or CW transmission is anticipated.

(3) RECEIVERS.—The receivers are mounted in a rack aft of the command transmitters, and are controlled by the receiver control box mounted on the base of the pilot's control stand. The receiver control box is

divided into three sections, each of which controls a receiver by means of electrical and mechanical connections. The receivers are turned on by means of a CW-OFF-MCW knob which in addition will (in the "CW" position) superimpose a tone on the continuous wave (unmodulated) signals received. Voice and tone modulated signals are received with the knob in the "MCW" position. Controls for adjustment of gain and tuning are also provided.

(4) ANTENNA.— The radio antenna consists of approximately one-half of the wire extending from an insulator, at the radio operator's station, to the top of the vertical stabilizer. The antenna is coupled to the receivers and transmitters by a transmit-receive transfer relay mounted above the command transmitter.

d. RADIO COMPASS.

(1) GENERAL.—The radio compass (SCR-269-G) consists in general of a receiver mounted in the upper left portion of the forward bomb bay, two control boxes, mounted at the copilot's and radio operator's stations, a "CW-VOICE" switch, mounted adjacent to the copilot's control box, a relay to switch control from one box to another, an automatic loop antenna located on the fuselage above the bomb bay, a retractable whip antenna aft of the forward upper turret, and direction indicators mounted in the pilot's instrument panel and in the radio operator's table. The latter indicator has a variation knob by which the radio operator may compensate for magnetic deviation and variation before obtaining a bearing.

(2) RECEIVER.

(*a*) The radio compass receiver is supplied 400-cycle 115-volt alternating current from the airplane's inverters, and has a frequency range of from 150 to 1750 kilocycles and may be operated employing either the loop antenna or the whip antenna, or both.

CAUTION

Do not extend whip antenna at air speeds in excess of 240 miles per hour.

(*b*) The radio compass may be operated from either of the two control boxes but not from both at the same time. The equipment is mechanically tuned from the boxes. Electrical control for either box is established by depressing the button marked "CONTROL" in the lower right-hand corner of the box. When control has been established a green light on the box will be illuminated. A tuning indicator is provided as an aid to precise tuning. Also, controls are available for manual loop control, receiver volume control, band change, and mode of operation. This last-mentioned switch has four positions, "OFF," "COMP," "ANT," and "LOOP."

(*c*) The "ANT" position is used when it is desired to receive aural signals with the whip antenna, as when receiving radio "range" signals. For best definition of these signals set the interphone volume knob fully clockwise and adjust receiver volume (AUDIO) for minimum usable.

(*d*) If reception on ANT is difficult due to precipitation static, LOOP reception may be employed with possibly better results. The loop antenna should be rotated by means of the LOOP L-R knob for maximum signal. For reception of radio range signals this will occur near 90-degree or 270-degree loop bearings. Adjust volume as under ANT reception.

NOTE

Cone of silence indications with LOOP operation are not always reliable. In some cases an increase instead of decrease in signal strength will be noted.

(*e*) The "LOOP" position may be used also in the "aural-null" direction finding method. The "AUDIO" knob may be used to vary the width of the "null" point. The tuning meter may be used as a visual null indication, if desired. When determining direction with this method it must be remembered that it is possible to obtain a null in a direction 180 degrees from the direction of signal reception.

(*f*) The "COMP" position is used for automatic direction finding. When so positioned, both the whip antenna and loop antenna are employed with the radio compass indicators showing a unidirectional bearing of the source of the radio signal received. This signal may also be heard in the operator's headphones.

e. MARKER BEACON.

(1) The marker beacon receiver is located below the center wing section and is designed to operate on ultra high frequency (75 mc.) signals. Its purpose is to indicate signals received from instrument landing markers, fan-type and cone of silence markers, and other facilities employing 75 mc. horizontally polarized radiation. The antenna is mounted below the fuselage between the bomb bays and is coupled to the receiver by a coaxial transmission line.

(2) As the airplane passes through the radiation field (conical) of a marker beacon transmitter, the amber indicator lamp in the pilot's instrument panel will flash in synchronism with the transmitter keying. Operation of this equipment is automatic, the only requirement being that the radio compass receiver must be "ON" to supply the power.

f. INTERPHONE.

(1) GENERAL.—The interphone system (RC 36) provides communication between crew members at 11 stations throughout the airplane. In addition the system allows crew members limited use of the radio facilities. The interphone jack boxes are provided for use by the following personnel: bombardier, pilot, copilot, engineer, navigator, radio operator, top gunner, side gunners (two), tail gunner, and relief crew (one).

(2) JACK BOX.

(*a*) Each jack box contains microphone and earphone jacks, a volume control knob, and a five-position selector knob. The selector knob positions are labeled: "COMP," "LIAISON," "COMMAND," "INTER," and "CALL."

(b) With the selector in the "COMP" position, the output of the radio compass receiver may be heard.

(c) With the selector on "LIAISON," the output of the liaison receiver and transmitter sidetone may be heard. The liaison transmitter (VOICE operation) may be modulated at the pilot's, copilot's, and radio operator's stations only.

(d) With the selector on "COMMAND" the command receiver output and transmitter sidetone may be heard. The command transmitter (VOICE operation) may be modulated at any of the interphone stations.

(e) With the selector on "INTER," communication is possible with all other interphone jack boxes and their selectors similarly positioned.

(f) With the selector in the "CALL" position the microphone output will override the radio outputs and will be heard at all stations without regard to the position of their selector switches. A spring is provided to prevent the selector from being inadvertently left in the "CALL" position.

(g) The volume control provides limited control over the outputs of the radio receivers only, no control being exerted over the output of the interphone amplifier.

(3) MICROPHONES.—T-30 throat microphones are furnished all stations. "Push-to-talk" microphone switches are located on the aileron control wheels for each pilot and in the ring sight for the top gunner. All other stations are provided with standard cord switches.

IMPORTANT

When using throat microphones, adjust the "buttons" to rest snugly on each side of the "Adam's apple." Speak distinctly and in a normal tone. Shouting will render speech unintelligible.

(4) AMPLIFIER. — The interphone amplifier is automatic in operation and is located on the shelf aft of the command radio receivers.

(5) DYNAMOTOR.—Amplifier plate voltage is supplied by a small dynamotor mounted adjacent to the amplifier. Inasmuch as there is no switch in either the amplifier or dynamotor, they will operate whenever the battery or generators are supplying power.

(6) FILTERS.—Filter switch boxes are mounted on the pilot's and copilot's oxygen panels. This filter is used to separate the weather (voice) signals from the range (1020-cycle tone) signals during their simultaneous transmission on the same frequency. The switch allows reception of weather signals only, beacon signals only, or both.

g. IFF RADIO (SCR-535-A OR SCR-695).

(1) Operation of this equipment is automatic. ON-OFF switches are located on the top of the pilot's instrument panel and in the IFF control box (BC 648).

(2) Two detonator switches are provided adjacent to the pilot's ON-OFF switch. Their purpose is to destroy the equipment if it is found necessary to abandon the airplane. When both push buttons are depressed together, a small charge is exploded in the receiver which is located below the radio operator's table. The explosion is confined within the receiver housing. No damage to the personnel or structure is anticipated; however, contact with the receiver should be avoided.

(3) An automatic detonator switch is provided adjacent to the IFF control box, at the radio operator's station. This switch may be set to destroy the receiver when subjected to severe shock, such as would be experienced in a crash. Operation of this switch should not be relied upon; however, every effort should be made to use the manual switch should the necessity arise.

(4) The fixed stub antenna is mounted on the forward bomb bay left-hand door.

NOTE

Regeneration adjustment of the IFF set must be made on the ground prior to take-off, to insure and correct operation of the equipment.

h. RADIO RECEIVING EQUIPMENT RC-103.

(1) The air-borne RC-103 equipment is designed to give lateral guidance to a pilot during landing operation. It includes a receiver, control box, antenna, and indicator. Power is obtained through a 10-ampere fuse in the turret junction shield.

(2) The RC-103 receiver is located on a shelf in the enclosed section aft of the pilot's seat, and is designed to operate at six tuned frequencies of 108.3, 108.7, 109.1, 109.5 109.9, and 10.3 megacycles. The receiver case back end is depressed to accommodate the dynamotor. Together, the unit functions as a mixer stage in which the incoming radio frequency is heterodyned with a frequency generated to produce the intermediate frequency. When the receiver is tuned to the field localizer transmitter a 90- and 150-cycle modulation will be audible in the head set while the indicator located on the pilot's instrument panel will reproduce the signals visually. Unless the aircraft's antenna is exactly ON COURSE the indicator needle will deflect to either the blue or the yellow side of the dial. If the indicator pointer is on the blue side of the indicator, the airplane is shown to be in the 90-cycle modulated blue area. Likewise, if the pointer is in the yellow area (150-cycle modulation) the aircraft is on the yellow side of the course. This is true regardless of the heading of the airplane so other references will have to be made to establish the correct heading when flying the localizer. A remote control box is provided at the pilot's station for monitoring the receiver, for tuning to any one of the six resonant frequencies, and for turning the receiver on or off. The monitoring circuit includes a volume control for adjusting the audio signal level in the operator's head set.

(3) A horseshoe shaped RC-103 antenna is supplied on the top of the fuselage above the wing center section.

i. OPERATING INSTRUCTIONS.

(1) RADIO NAVIGATION VARIABLES.

(a) When using radio equipment for navigational purposes it must be remembered that, although the equipment may be operating satisfactorily, erroneous indications may be obtained as the result of the following conditions:

1. Night effect or reflection of the radio wave from the sky is always present. It may be recognized by a fluctuation in bearings or by signal fading. The remedy is:

a. Increase altitude, thereby increasing the strength of the direct wave.

b. Take an average of the fluctuations or select a lower frequency station.

c. Night effect is worst at sunrise and sunset. Night effect may be present on stations at 1750 kilocycles at distances greater than 20 miles; as the frequency decreases, the distance increases, until, at 200 kilocycles the the distance will be about 200 miles. Satisfactory bearings, however, will often be obtained at much greater distances than stated above, and sometimes unsatisfactory bearings may be obtained at shorter distances.

2. The presence of mountain ranges, rivers, and the like will cause the patterns of the transmitter to be uneven and somewhat scalloped. This will produce erroneous or fluctuating bearings or multiple on-course signals which will sound exactly like the true on-course signals except that they will usually be bounded by identical quadrant letters. In some cases the multiple will be like the true course or even with reversed signals.

3. The presence of a bend in a radio range quadrant leg is due to the same topographical irregularities which cause multiples.

4. When a radio wave travels through a cold front, erroneous and fluctuating bearings may result to a limited extent.

5. Station interference between two or more stations on the same frequency may result in erroneous indications. Clear channel stations are always preferable. If clear channel stations cannot be used as a reference, a stable station widely separated by distance from other stations on the same frequency is desirable.

6. Where a radio range signal crosses an irregularity in terrain, such as a deep canyon, there may exist a false cone of silence. As the radio waves pass over such an irregularity, some of the waves will be reflected back from the far wall. The reflected waves serve to cancel the direct waves when over the canyon, and cause the signal to disappear momentarily. False cones may change in character at different times of day. Additional Heaviside reflection may obscure the false cone at night. A true cone of silence produces a definite increase in volume just before entering and just after leaving the cone. The quadrant signal to the right after emerging from a true cone of silence is not the same as that received before entering the cone.

7. For the best definition of A-N radio quadrant signals the interphone jack box "INCREASE OUTPUT" control must be in a fully clockwise position, and the head-set volume level should then be adjusted by means of the control box volume control in accordance with the following considerations:

a. At extremely low volume levels which are just above the threshold of audibility, the ear can not easily distinguish differences in the volume of the "A" and "N" signals. When flying on the edge of the on-course it is very desirable to detect small differences between the "A" and "N" signals. Consequently, the volume level should be set high enough to give a loud but not unpleasant signal.

b. Radio set SCR-274-N and radio compass SCR-269 have delayed automatic gain control provisions incorporated in their design. This can be stated as a feature providing for a fixed output level effective only after a predetermined high level has been reached through clockwise adjustment of the control box volume control. When the AVC feature is active, true representation of "A" and "N" signal input is not possible, and errors may be introduced into radio range navigation.

c. In view of the above considerations it can be seen that the head-set volume level should be adjusted to a minimum usable. This can be determined by listening to a signal which is slightly off the "on-course" zone and adjusting the head-set volume to give the best audible ratio between signals.

d. It can be seen from the above discussion of variables that the question of accuracy of radio navigational equipment indications should, if possible, be subjected to a check against navigation data obtained by other means.

(2) PILOT'S AND COPILOT'S POSITION.

(a) GENERAL—OPERATING INSTRUCTIONS.

1. If the airplane is not in flight, either an external source of power or the auxiliary power plant must be used to supply power for operation of the communications equipment. A standard three-prong, external power receptacle is installed in the aft wall of the No. 2 nacelle wheel well (figure 67) for plugging in the power supply from a portable generator. When using an external source of power, battery and ignition switches must be in "OFF" position.

2. The auxiliary power plant is installed aft of the rear pressurized cabin on the port side. (See figure 2.) To start auxiliary power plant:

a. Place throttle lever (figure 68-3) in "IDLE" position.

b. Place auxiliary power plant ignition switch (figure 69-4) "ON."

c. Place generator switch (figure 68-2) in "START" position.

d. As soon as the auxiliary power plant starts firing place generator switch in "OFF" position. When the power plant oil gage indicates operating temperature, move throttle to "RUN" and generator switch to "ON." If engine or engines are running turn equalizer switch to "ON."

e. Place double throw "EMERGENCY" ignition switches (figure 43) and battery switch (figure 13) "ON."

f. When operation of the radio compass is desired, the a-c inverter switch (figure 13) must be "ON" to furnish the a-c power necessary for the operation of the loop-drive components of the equipment. When operation of the communications equipment is completed turn off these switches and turn off auxiliary power unit.

3. PLUG HEAD SET into head-set disconnector cord jack. (See figure 69-3.) (This cord extends from filter switch box.) PLUG THE THROAT MICROPHONE into microphone disconnector cord jack. (See figure 69-9.) (Cord must be plugged into the interphone jack-box "MIC" jack as in figure 69-1.)

4. Set the interphone jack-box (figure 69-4) selector switch on the applicable position and turn the "INCREASE OUTPUT" knob fully clockwise.

5. Set filter switch box (figure 69-2) selector switch on "BOTH." If rejection of radio range quadrant signals is desired, set on "VOICE." If reception of radio range quadrant signals with rejection of voice modulation is desired set on "RANGE."

(b) TO OPERATE INTERPHONE
TYPE RC-36.

1. The interphone amplifier is in operation when an external power plant is being used or when battery and ignition switches are on. (Audio output of the command receivers, compass receiver, and liaison receiver can be heard over the interphone system without the interphone amplifier being operative, but no output over the interphone system when on either "INTER" or "CALL" will be heard, unless the interphone amplifier is energized.)

2. Hold the interphone jack-box selector switch (figure 69-4) in "CALL" position, call desired crew member, and release selector switch, allowing it to return to "INTER."

3. When the crew member answers, intercommunication may be carried on with the selector switch on "INTER."

NOTE

The interphone jack-box volume control provides limited control over the outputs of all positions except "INTER" and "CALL."

4. On the aisle stand between the pilot and copilot is located a phone call switch. (See figure 12.) In the aft pressurized compartments there is a call light mounted by each interphone jack box. By use of the phone call switch the pilot can signal the crew members in these compartments to listen on interphone.

(c) ADJUSTMENT OF THROAT
MICROPHONE TYPE T-30.

1. The throat microphone neck band length should be adjusted to allow the microphone elements to bear firmly but not tightly against the throat. For best

Figure 69—Pilot's Radio Controls

1. Microphone Plug-in
2. Filter Switch Box
3. Head-Set Extension Cord
4. Interphone Jack Box
5. Command Receiver Control Box will be installed here on later airplanes
6. Command Receiver Control Box
7. Command Transmitter Control Box
8. "PUSH-TO-TALK" Switch
9. Microphone Extension Cord Clip

results the microphone elements should be equally spaced about the "Adam's apple." Do not allow clothing to get between the microphone elements and the skin of the wearer. Speak in a normal tone of voice.

(d) TO OPERATE COMMAND RADIO
SET—SCR-274-N.

1. RECEIVING COMPONENTS.

a. Set the three "A-B" switches on the receiver control box (figure 69-6) to "A." These switches have no function in this installation on "B" position.

b. Select section of the receiver control box covering the desired frequency band.

c. Turn the "CW-OFF-MCW" switch to the type of reception desired.

d. Turn tuning crank to desired station frequency.

e. Set head-set volume to desired level by adjusting the "INCREASE OUTPUT" knob.

NOTE

Two or more frequencies, each peculiar to one receiver, may be monitored at one time by appropriate adjustment of head-set volume levels.

f. To turn off receiver throw "CW-OFF-MCW" switch to "OFF."

2. TRANSMITTING COMPONENTS.

a. Monitor the frequency of desired answering station before transmission is effected.

b. Turn "TRANSPOWER" switch on transmitter control box, (figure 69-7) "ON."

c. Set frequency selector switch to the desired frequency as indicated on placard above switch.

d. Set the "TONE-CW-VOICE" switch to the type of emission desired.

e. If "TONE" or "CW" emission is selected, transmit with "PUSH-TO-TALK" switch (figure 69-8) on the control wheel.

f. If "VOICE" emission was selected, transmit by pressing the "PUSH-TO-TALK" switch on the control wheel and speaking slowly and distinctly in a normal tone of voice.

g. If for any reason the hand microphone type T-17 is used, make sure the protruding knurled nut at "MIC" jack is turned fully counterclockwise and left in that position as long as T-17 remains in use.

h. During flight the "TRANSPOWER" switch on the transmitter control box is usually kept "ON" to keep the transmitter tube filaments warm and ready for instant use and also to keep interphone dynamotor operating. The emission selector switch should always be kept on "VOICE" position except when it is desired to transmit code, as in the "CW" and "MCW" positions the dynamotor is running continuously, resulting in dynamotor overheating and consequent equipment failures. In "VOICE" position the dynamotor runs only when the "PRESS-TO-TALK" switch is closed.

i. In the event of interphone equipment failure the audio frequency section of the command transmitter may be substituted for the regular interphone amplifier. To make this connection the pilot should place his command transmitter control box channel selector switch in either No. "3" or No. "4" position. (See figure 69-7.) Set interphone jack-box selector switches on "COMMAND" and operate as if selector switches were on "INTER."

NOTE

In this position it is not possible to establish communication with ground station or any aircraft. To resume normal command set operation place channel selector switch back in either No. "1" or "2" position.

j. To turn off transmitter, throw "TRANS-POWER" switch to "OFF."

(e) TO OPERATE RADIO COMPASS SCR-269.

1. GENERAL.

a. This equipment provides for:

(1) Aural reception of modulated or unmodulated radio frequency energy, using a nondirectional antenna, when operating on the "ANT" position of the selector switch.

(2) Aural reception (at a net gain of snow static reduction and a loss of signal strength as compared to operation on "ANT") of modulated or unmodulated radio frequency energy, using a shielded loop antenna, when operating on the "LOOP" position of the selector switch.

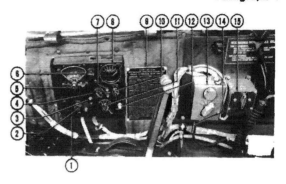

Figure 70—Copilot's Radio Controls

1. Radio Compass Control Box
2. Tuning Crank
3. Control Indicator Light
4. Volume Control
5. Band Change Switch
6. "LIGHTS" Control
7. Spare Lamps
8. Tuning Meter
9. Chart MC-238
10. Loop L-R Switch
11. Function Selector Switch
12. "CONTROL" Push-Button Switch
13. Interphone Jack Box
14. Microphone Jack (Disconnector Cord)
15. Filter Switch Box

(3) Aural null directional indications of the arrival of modulated or unmodulated radio frequency energy, using a loop antenna, when operating on the "LOOP" position of the selector switch.

(4) Automatic bearing indication, with regard to the longitudinal axis of the airplane, of the direction of arrival of radio frequency energy and simultaneous aural reception of modulated or unmodulated radio frequency energy, when operating on the "COMP" position of the selector switch.

b. When using the radio compass as a homing device, the indications are such that the aircraft will ultimately arrive over the radio station antenna regardless of probable drift due to cross-wind. However, the flight path will be a curved line, and coordination with ground fixes or landing fields along the route will be either difficult or impossible. Consequently, it is often expedient to fly a straight-line course by offsetting the aircraft's heading to compensate for wind drift. To do this, determine the wind drift, either with a drift sight or by noting the change in magnetic compass reading over a period of time, while homing with the radio compass.

c. Complete the necessary operations included in 2. *a.*

d. If airplane is not in flight, turn on inverter selector switch (engineer's station) and when operation of the radio set is completed, turn this switch off.

e. This operating procedure may be performed at either the copilot's or radio operator's positions. To assume control at either position, the selector switch (figure 70-11) on either radio compass control box must be turned to the type of operation desired and the "CONTROL" button (figure 70-12) must be pressed until the green control indicator lamp (figure 70-3) lights. An I-82-A type compass indicator (figure 74-19) is mounted in the radio operator's table. If copilot desires to obtain a radio fix, it will be desirable to have radio operator compensate for magnetic deviation and variation and take the bearing readings with the I-82-A compass indicator.

f. Dial lamps may be turned on and their brilliance controlled by means of the "LIGHTS" control on the compass control box. (See figure 70-6.)

g. Head-set volume may be regulated by means of the "AUDIO" control. (See figure 70-4.)

h. Select station frequency with band selector switch and tuning crank. Move tuning crank to a position producing greatest clockwise indication of tuning meter. The tuning meter (figure 70-8) should not be construed to be a distance indicator.

i. Provision is made for aural reception of "CW" signals. Control of this feature is provided by the "CW-VOICE" switch on the panel of the radio compass receiver and by the remote "CW-VOICE" switch adjacent to the copilot's compass control box. With the "CW-VOICE" switch in "VOICE" position the compass and homing components of this equipment will function properly while receiving "CW" signals, but aural identification of such signals will be impossible unless the "CW-VOICE" switch is set on "CW."

2. To operate as a receiver only, using the non-directional fixed sense antenna:

a. Set the selector switch (figure 70-11) on "ANT."

b. Set band selector switch to desired band and tune in desired station by means of tuning crank, making final adjustment by referring to tuning meter.

c. Regulate the head-set volume by adjusting "AUDIO" control.

NOTE

If reception on "ANT" is noisy due to precipitation static, commonly known as rain or snow static, operate on shielded loop antenna. Precipitation static existing in air mass fronts at different temperatures can sometimes be avoided by crossing the front at right angles, and then proceeding on the desired course, instead of flying along the air mass front.

d. To turn off radio compss, turn selector switch on compass control box to "OFF."

3. To operate as a receiver only, utilizing the shielding provision of the loop antenna to reduce precipitation static noises:

a. Set the selector switch on "LOOP."

b. Tune in desired station.

c. Depress "LOOP L-R" knob (figure 70-10) on the radio compass control box and turn it to "L" or "R," rotating loop to obtain maximum signal strength as indicated by head-set volume. Release "LOOP L-R" knob and make final adjustment of loop position at slow

speed by turning the knob to "L" or "R." Changing course will affect signal strength and necessitate readjustment of the loop position.

d. Regulate head-set volume with "AUDIO" knob.

NOTE

If the loop is in null (minimum signal) position when flying on a radio range course, the signal may fade in and out and possibly be mistaken for a cone of silence. When operating on "LOOP," cone of silence indications from radio range stations employing loop-type radiators (shown on radio facility chart) are not reliable. The signal may increase in volume to a strong surge when directly over the station instead of indicating a silent zone.

e. To turn off radio compass, turn the selector switch on compass control box to "OFF."

4. To operate as an aural null homing device, utilizing the directional characteristics of the loop antenna:

a. Set the selector switch on "LOOP."

b. Tune in desired (preferable clear channel) station.

c. If compass indicator pointer (figure 39-0) mounted on pilot's instrument panel is not at zero, depress the "LOOP L-R" knob and turn it to "L" or "R" position until the pointer rests on zero. Final adjustment of loop position can be made at slow speed by releasing "LOOP L-R" knob and turning it to the "L" or "R."

d. Turn the "AUDIO" control fully clockwise and head airplane in proper direction, based upon the null (point where a sharp minimum or loss of signal is found) indicated in the head set. (The broadness of the null depends on the strength of the signal. Strong signals produce very sharp nulls, sometimes as small as one-tenth of a degree.) Vary "AUDIO" control until the null is of satisfactory width. The tuning meter may be used as a visual null indicator.

NOTE

When determining direction of flight by this method, it must be remembered that a 180-degree ambiguity exists, in that the airplane may be flying either directly TOWARD or directly AWAY FROM the station. If the direction of flight with regard to this ambiguity is not known and the radio compass is inoperative on the "COMP" position, a standard orientation procedure will have to be executed before flying any great distance along the null.

e. To turn off radio compass, turn selector switch on compass control box to "OFF."

5. To operate as a homing compass, utilizing the unidirectional characteristics of the radio compass when operating with both the sense and loop antennae.

a. Set the selector switch on "COMP."

b. Tune in desired station.

c. Apply rudder in direction shown by radio compass indicator (figure 39-0) until the pointer centers on zero. This indication is unidirectional; as long as pointer rests on zero the airplane is headed toward the transmitting antenna of the radio station.

d. Regulate head-set volume by adjusting "AUDIO" control.

e. Since a pronounced AVC action may be present when operating the radio compass on "COMP," aural indications received on this position should *not* be used when homing on a radio range station.

f. To turn off radio compass, turn selector switch on the compass control box to "OFF."

6. To operate as a direction finder for the purpose of establishing a fix.

a. GENERAL.

(1) The usual method of establishing a fix is by triangular plotting of three bearings obtained on three radio stations. Prior to making fix determinations, stations to be used should be located on a map, tuned in, identified, and dial reading logged. This avoids delay and error at the time of obtaining the fix.

(2) For best accuracy several bearings should be taken in rapid succession thereby eliminating error caused by the distance traveled between bearing observations. Bearings cannot be accurate unless the aircraft is held on a steady heading.

(3) When close to a station, accurate bearings cannot be taken with the aircraft in a steep bank. This is especially applicable to reception of signals from instrument landing trucks.

(4) Only head-on bearings are entirely dependable. If side bearings are taken, keep the wings horizontal.

(5) Do not depend on two stations for a fix of location; at least three station bearings should be used. In general a set of stations with bearings spaced at approximately equal intervals throughout 360 degrees will give best accuracy.

(6) In compensating for magnetic variation (declination), it must be remembered that the variation indicated on the geographic compass rose (printed on the map) of the radio station on which the bearing is being taken is the figure normally used. The magnetic variation of the locality over which the airplane is flying at the time the bearing is taken is not generally known. However, if this figure is used, the station compass rose variation figure should be excluded. In obtaining bearing for plotting on radio direction finding maps (D. F. maps), the variation should be excluded from the computation, as the compass roses on these charts are offset to compensate for magnetic variation.

b. AUTOMATIC VISUAL DIRECTION FINDING.

(1) With the radio compass selector switch on "COMP," tune the first station, previously logged and identified, and record the reciprocal reading of radio compass indicator pointer on pilot's instrument panel, which is the station-to-airplane bearing.

(2) Rapidly repeat operation (1) to obtain two additional station-to-airplane bearings.

(3) To the station-to-airplane bearing obtained in (1), *add* the magnetic compass heading of the airplane (referring to the compass correction card attached to the magnetic compass in order to obtain a true magnetic heading).

NOTE

If radio operator is taking the bearing, he may compensate for the magnetic deviation and variation on the I-82-A indicator before obtaining the bearing.

(4) Refer to the air navigation chart and obtain the magnetic variation (declination) for the locality of the radio station involved in operation (1).

(5) If the magnetic variation for the locality is shown as easterly, *add* the indicated amount of variation to the result of operation (3). If the variation is shown as westerly, *subtract* the indicated amount of variation from the result of operation (3).

NOTE

When using direction finding (D. F.) maps, omit operations (4) and (5) as the compass roses surrounding the geographical locations of the radio stations are offset to compensate for magnetic variations.

(6) If the resultant sum of operation (5) is larger than 360 degrees, subtract 360 degrees from the result of operation (5) to obtain the correct station-to-airplane bearing. Plot this result on the map. (See figure 71.)

(7) With each of the two additional station-to-airplane bearings obtained in (2), repeat operations (3), (4), (5), and (6), using the bearings obtained in operation (2) in each case.

(8) When the three bearings are plotted on a map at the proper angle, indicated by the compass roses, the lines should intersect. This point of intersection is the approximate location of the airplane at time of observation. (See figure 71.)

c. AURAL NULL DIRECTION FINDING.

(1) Set the selector switch on "LOOP."

(2) Tune in desired (preferable clear channel) station.

(3) Turn "AUDIO" control fully clockwise, *depress* "LOOP L-R" knob and turn it to "L" or "R," rotating loop in proper direction to null position indicated by minimum head set signal volume or tuning meter dip. Release "LOOP L-R" knob and make final adjustment of loop position at slow speed by turning knob to "L" or "R."

(4) Record the station-to-airplane bearing indicated by reciprocal reading of radio compass indicator pointer.

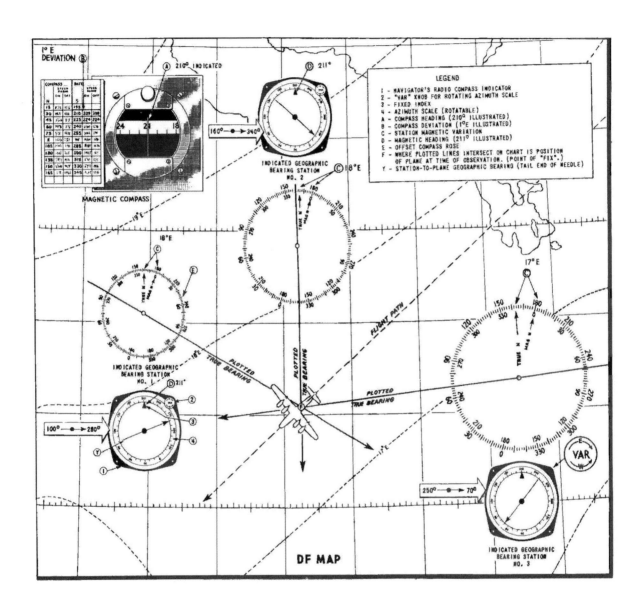

*Figure 71—Plotting Radio Compass Bearings
to Obtain a Fix*

(5) Rapidly repeat operations (2), (3), and (4) in order to obtain two additional station-to-airplane bearings.

(6) To the station-to-airplane bearing obtained in operation (4), *add* the magnetic compass heading of the airplane (referring to the compass correction card attached to the magnetic compass, in order to obtain a true magnetic heading).

(7) Refer to the air navigation chart and obtain magnetic variation (declination) for locality of radio station involved in operation (4).

(8) If magnetic variation for locality. is shown as easterly, *add* indicated amount of variation to result of operation (6). If variation is shown as westerly, *subtract* indicated amount of variation from result of operation (6).

NOTE

When using direction finding (D. F.) maps, omit operations (7) and (8) as compass roses surrounding the geographical locations of radio stations are offset to compensate for magnetic variation.

(9) If resultant sum of operation (8) is larger than 360 degrees, subtract 360 degrees from result of operation (8) to obtain correct station-to-airplane bearing. Plot this result on map.

(10) With each of two additional station-to-airplane bearings obtained in operation (5), repeat operations (6), (7), (8), and (9), using bearings obtained in operation (5) in each case.

(11) When the three bearings are plotted on a map at the proper angle, indicated by compass roses, lines should intersect. This point of intersection is approximate location of airplane at time of observation. (See figure 71.)

(12) Bearings obtained by aural - null method are subject to 180 degrees ambiguity. Where 180 degrees ambiguity exists, the bearing lines plotted on the map will indicate an airplane-to-station (rather than a station-to-airplane) bearing and they will fail to intersect. When it is clearly evident that 180 degrees ambiguity exists, the reciprocal bearing may be plotted. In other cases of doubtful correctness the bearing may be retaken.

(13) To turn off radio compass, turn selector switch on the compass control box to "OFF."

(f) TO OPERATE MARKER BEACON RECEIVER RC-43.

1. Turn on radio compass which furnishes power for marker beacon receiver.

2. When flying over an airway fan marker or "Z" (cone of silence) marker (indicated on radio facility chart) or an instrument landing marker, the indicator lamp (figure 39) will light.

3. The interval during which the marker beacon indicator lamp will be lit varies from a few seconds to as long as several minutes, depending upon the type of marker, as well as the altitude and speed of the airplane. Cone of silence markers utilize nondirectional antenna arrays which cause equal indications for any direction of flight. Indications over cone of silence markers last about 1 minute at 10,000 feet altitude, when the speed of the airplane is 150 miles per hour.

4. When passing over a marker the indication should be steady or flash regularly, following the keying of the transmitter. Cone of silence markers and Army instrument landing markers are not keyed. Fan-type markers and C. A. A. instrument landing markers are identified by keying. The radio receiver may not follow the keying of the 100-watt fan marker transmitters when the airplane is passing through the strongest part of the beam at low altitudes.

5. To turn marker beacon receiver off, turn off radio compass.

(g) TO OPERATE RECEIVING EQUIPMENT RC-103-A.

1. GENERAL.

a. Radio receiving equipment RC-103-A to be installed is air-borne equipment designed to give lateral guidance to a pilot during landing operations. Vertical guidance is accomplished by use of barometric altimeter readings over marker beacon stations, or by use of a glide path system which is being developed.

b. Radio receiver BC-733-A operates at six fixed crystal-controlled tuned frequencies of 108.3, 108.7, 109.1, 109.5, 109.9, and 110.3 megacycles. At the present only three crystals are being installed. Incoming signals operate indicator I-101-( ) which indicates to a pilot whether the airplane is to the right, to the left, or on course over the landing strip. I-101-( ) does not indicate the heading of the airplane. The receiver also delivers audio frequency power to the head sets simultaneously.

2. RECEIVER OPERATING TEST.

a. Place interphone jack box selector switch on "COMMAND" and turn volume control fully clockwise.

b. Turn volume control on radio control box BC-732-A to about midscale and turn "ON-OFF" switch to "ON."

c. The dynamotor should start immediately and after a few moments a noise, characteristic of a high gain radio receiver, should be audible in the headphones.

d. Operate the selector switch on the control box to the letter corresponding to a nearby localizer transmitter, if one exists. The 90- and 150-cycle modulation should immediately become audible in the head set, and unless the airplane is exactly on the course, the indicator should deflect to the right or left.

(h) TO OPERATE LIAISON RADIO SET SCR-287-A.

1. GENERAL.—The liaison radio set may be operated from the pilot's and copilot's position only after operating adjustments have been accomplished at the radio operator's position.

2. RECEIVING AND TRANSMITTING
COMPONENTS.

a. Instruct radio operator to make operating adjustments of liaison receiver and transmitter.

b. Set the interphone jack box on "LIAISON" and receive and transmit by conventional use of head set, "INCREASE OUTPUT" control (on interphone jack box), and the microphone.

c. When communication is finished, instruct radio operator to turn off equipment and, if necessary, to reel in trailing antenna.

(i) OPERATION OF IFF RADIO SET SCR-595
OR SCR-695.

1. OPERATING COMPONENTS.

a. Turn "ON-OFF" switch on the IFF control box at the radio operator's position or at the pilot's position (figure 72-2) to "ON."

b. Set selector switch on control box to numbered position designated by tactical orders.

c. If "EMERGENCY" operation is desired, place "EMERGENCY" switch (figure 72-3) on control box to "ON."

d. To turn off the radio set, turn the "ON-OFF" switch to "OFF."

2. DESTRUCTOR COMPONENTS.—If necessary to destroy the IFF radio set, simultaneously press two switch buttons (figure 72-1) on the destructor switch.

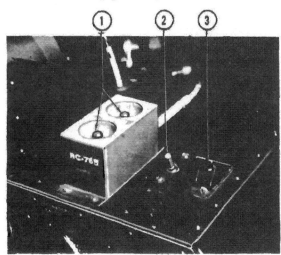

**Figure 72—IFF Control Switches Above
Pilot's Instrument Panel**

1. IFF Destructor Switches
2. IFF Power Switch
3. IFF Emergency Switch

NOTE

The above switch is paralleled by an automatic inertia-type switch which is mechanically energized by a crash landing.

(j) OPERATION OF PORTABLE
EMERGENCY RADIO TRANSMITTER
TYPE SCR-578-A.

1. GENERAL.

a. A complete self-contained portable emergency transmitter is provided for operation anywhere away from the airplane. Primarily designed for use in a small boat or life raft, it may be placed in operation anywhere. The unit is equipped with a small parachute to permit dropping from airplane in event of an emergency.

b. When operated, the transmitter emits an "MCW" signal and is pretuned to the international distress frequency of 500 kilocycles. Automatic transmission of a predetermined signal is provided. Any searching party can home on the signal with the aid of a radio compass.

c. No receiver is provided.

2. REMOVAL FROM AIRPLANE.

a. If the airplane has made an emergency landing on water, the emergency set should be removed at the same time that the life raft is removed. The set is waterproof and will float; therefore, it is not necessary to take any precautions in keeping the equipment out of the water. Be sure that it does not float out of reach.

b. The emergency set may be dropped from the airplane by use of the parachute attached. The altitude of the airplane when dropping the equipment should be between 300 and 500 feet. To drop the equipment, the following steps should be observed:

c. Tie the loose end of the parachute static line to any solid metal structure of the airplane.

CAUTION

Be sure the static line is in clear and will not foul.

d. Throw the emergency set out through a convenient opening in airplane. Parachute will be opened by static line.

CAUTION

Do not attach static line to any part of one's body when throwing the equipment through the opening.

3. OPERATION.—Complete operating instructions are contained in one of the bags which contain the equipment. Complete instructions for the use of transmitter are also located on the transmitter.

(3) RADIO OPERATOR'S POSITION.

(a) GENERAL.—TO OPERATE COMMUNICATIONS EQUIPMENT.

1. Plug head-set into head-set disconnector cord (cord must be plugged into the interphone jack box (figure 73-15) PHONES jack). *Plug throat* microphone, or hand microphone, if installed, into microphone disconnector cord jack (cord must be plugged into the interphone jack box "MIC" jack). (See figure 73-16.)

2. Set the interphone jack-box (figure 73-14) selector switch on applicable position and turn IN-CREASE OUTPUT KNOB fully clockwise. If listening to radio sets having operating controls at other positions, head-set volume may be regulated with INCREASE OUTPUT knob.

3. See paragraph (2) *(a)* for operation of auxiliary power plant or external power.

(b) TO OPERATE INTERPHONE.

1. Complete necessary operations included in (3) *(a)*, preceding.

2. Hold selector switch on the interphone jack box in the "CALL" position, call desired crew member, and release selector switch, allowing it to return to "INTER."

3. When the crew member answers, intracommunication may be carried on with selector switch on "INTER."

(c) TO OPERATE COMMAND RADIO SET
—SCR-274-N.

1. This radio set may be operated from this position only after operating adjustments have been made by the pilot.

2. Set the interphone jack box selector switch on the "COMMAND" position and receive and transmit by conventional use of the head set and the microphone.

(d) TO OPERATE RADIO COMPASS—SCR-269-G.—The radio compass may be operated by the radio operator or the copilot. At the radio operator's position there is a control box (figure 73-10) and an azimuth scale indicator (figure 73-19) which may be corrected for deviation and variation prior to obtaining a bearing. The instructions under paragraph (2) *(e)* apply to operation of the radio compass from the radio operator's position.

(e) TO OPERATE LIAISON RADIO SET—
SCR-287-( ).

1. GENERAL.

a. Only those instructions necessary to enable crew members, other than the radio operator to operate this set in case of nonavailability of abbreviated instructions, referred to in the following paragraph, have been included herein. It is assumed that considerably more efficient operation, based upon a more extensive knowledge of the use of the equipment, can be attained by the radio operator.

b. It is recommended that these instructions be supplemented by abbreviated instructions and a chart showing all transmitter and antenna loading unit dial and switch settings for each frequency normally used. Dial and switch settings listed should be applicable to a given installation in a given airplane and should be based upon flight operating tests. These abbreviated instructions should be available to crew members who may be required to operate the equipment.

2. RECEIVING COMPONENTS.

a. RADIO RECEIVER, BC-348-( ).

(1) Complete the necessary operations included in (3) *(a)* preceding.

(2) Turn "OFF-AVC-MVC" switch on the liaison receiver (figure 73-4) to the "MVC" position.

(3) Turn the "CW-OSC" "ON-OFF" switch to "ON."

(4) Turn "BEAT FREQ" control so arrow on knob is pointing upward.

(5) Turn "CRYSTAL OUT-IN" switch to "OUT."

(6) Turn "DIAL LIGHTS" control clockwise.

(7) Turn "INCREASE VOL" control clockwise until a sufficiently strong background is heard.

(8) Turn "BAND SWITCH" to band covering 500 kilocycles, indicated on the frequency dial above the switch.

(9) Tune receiver to signal nearest to 500 kilocycles by means of the tuning crank.

(10) Tune the "ANT ALIGN" control for maximum signal indicated by head-set volume.

NOTE

In absence of signal the proper adjustment can be judged by the loudness of the background noise.

(11) To receive a modulated signal, turn "CW OSC" switch to "OFF."

(12) Tune in desired signal by means of band change switch, tuning crank, and volume control.

(13) If a CW signal is being received, signal pitch may be adjusted by "BEAT FREQ" control.

(14) Automatic volume control may be employed after signal is tuned in by turning the "AVC-OFF-MVC" switch to "AVC."

(15) If noise and interfering signal reduction is desired, turn the "CRYSTAL OUT-IN" switch to the "IN" position and make any tuning adjustments necessary.

(16) Auxiliary head-set jacks marked "TEL" are provided on the face of the receiver.

(17) To turn off the receiver, turn the "AVC-OFF-MVC" switch to the "OFF" position.

3. TRANSMITTING COMPONENTS.

a. GENERAL.

(1) The transmitter may be expected to give satisfactory service on "CW" as long as cabin altitude is less than 27,000 feet. On "TONE" and "VOICE," however, insulation break-down may be experienced with transmitter tuning unit TU-8-( ) (6200-7700 kilocycles) above cabin altitude of 25,000 feet, and with tuning unit TU-9-( ) (7700-10,000 kilocycles) above a cabin altitude of 19,000 feet. These altitude limitations may be exceeded slightly by care in tuning and by carefully guard-

Figure 73—Radio Operator's Station

1. Two of the Seven Transmitter Tuning Units
2. Liaison Dynamotor
3. Liaison Transmitter, BC-375-( )
4. Liaison Receiver, BC-348-H
5. Antenna Transfer Switch
6. Antenna Tuning Unit, BC-306-A
7. Reading Light and Switch
8. Command Transmitters
9. Command Receivers
10. Radio Compass Control Box
11. Extension Trouble Lamp
12. Compass Chart
13. Inertia Switch (IFF)
14. Interphone Jack Box
15. Head-Set Disconnector Cord Plugged in Phones Jack
16. Microphone Disconnector Cord Plugged in Mic Jack
17. Antenna Reel Control Box
18. Transmitting Key
19. Compass Indicator 1-82A Mounted Beneath a Shield at This Point
20. Trailing Antenna Fair-lead Control Lever
21. Microphone Push-to-Talk Switch

ing against accumulation of dust and other foreign matter in the equipment. Complete assurance of effective operation between 6200 and 10,000 kilocycles at cabin altitudes between 19,000 and 27,000 feet may be had on "CW" alone. Transmitter tuning unit TU-26-( ) may be expected to give satisfactory service at all cabin altitudes up to 15,000 feet.

(2) Inasmuch as operation of the liaison transmitter on frequencies below 800 kilocycles involves tuning instructions for the antenna tuning unit (figure 73-6), the tuning instructions for the transmitter are given under two sections, viz, for frequencies above 800 kilocycles and for frequencies below 800 kilocycles.

b. To operate liaison transmitter on frequencies above 800 kilocycles.

(1) Monitor the desired frequency on the receiver before effecting transmission.

(2) Insert the transmitter tuning unit covering the desired frequency in the transmitter. (See figure 73-3.) Two tuning units (figure 73-1) are mounted under the operator's table and four are mounted on the port side adjacent to the top turret in rear pressurized compartment.

(3) Set the "BAND CHANGE SWITCH" (A) on the position indicated on the "Calibration Chart" on the face of the tuning unit installed.

(4) Set the "M. O. TUNING" control (B) on the dial calibration (last two figures indicated on the vernier) corresponding to the desired frequency and the Calibration Chart. If the frequency falls between listed frequencies on Calibration Chart, see paragraph 3.f. for interpolation instructions.

(5) Set the "P. A. TUNING" control (C) on the dial calibration corresponding to the desired frequency and the Calibration Chart.

(6) Set the "ANT. COUPLING SWITCH" (D) on position "2."

(7) Set the "ANT. IND. TUNING" control (M) on "ZERO."

(8) Set the "ANT. CIRCUIT SWITCH" (N) on "2."

(9) Set the "ANT. CAP. TUNING" control (O) on "50."

(10) Set the "ANT. IND. SWITCH" (P) on "1."

(11) Set the variometer switch "E" on the antenna tuning unit (figure 73-6) on position "1."

(12) Disconnect the antenna from the transmitter by throwing the antenna transfer switch (figure 73-5) to an "OPEN" position.

(13) Set the "TONE-CW-VOICE" switch on "CW."

(14) Set the "CW FIL.—MOD. FIL." switch on "CW FIL."

(15) If the airplane is in flight, request pilot's permission to reel out antenna.

NOTE

The trailing antenna must be in before landing, when flying in formation or when not in use.

(16) To reel out antenna, place trailing antenna fair-lead control lever (figure 73-20) in "OUT" position and antenna transfer switch in trailing antenna position.

NOTE

If the trailing wire antenna control box (figure 73-17) indicator does not read "000," adjust by means of the reset knob on left side of control box.

(17) Turn the "OFF-IN-OUT" switch on antenna reel control box to the "OUT" position and reel out an appropriate number of turns based upon the following table. One turn, indicated on the meter, equals approximately one foot.

RECOMMENDED ANTENNA LENGTHS:

Kilocycle	¼ Wave Lengths (Feet)	¾ Wave Lengths (Feet)
2000	123	
3000	82	
4000	62	
5000	49	147
6000	41	123
7000	35	105
8000	31	93
9000	27	81
10000	24	73

For frequencies below 800 kilocycles, use full length of trailing antenna.

(18) Turn the "ON-OFF" switch to "ON." Note filament voltage indicated on "FIL. VOLTAGE" meter. The pointer should fall on the red line. If not, remove the tube shield (upper front panel) and make sure the "24-28.5-VOLT" switch is in the appropriate position (if operating equipment from a battery cart as an external source of power, use the "24-VOLT" position; if the auxiliary power plant, or external power plant, or the engines are running and delivering rated generator voltage output, use the "28.5-VOLT" position which is the normal terminal voltage of a battery under charge). Check to see that the "A-C—D-C" switch in the tube compartment is in the "D-C" position.

NOTE

Do not change tubes or make adjustments inside the transmitter with the test key, the microphone switch, or the hand key depressed. Do not operate any equipment with the tube shield removed.

(19) Press the "TEST KEY" on the face of the transmitter and tune the "P. A. TUNING" control "C" to obtain the minimum value of plate current, indicated on the "TOTAL PL. CURRENT" meter.

NOTE

If the .ninimum total plate current exceeds 100 milliamperes with the antenna circuit open, the transmitter should not be operated until the defect is corrected by maintenance personnel. Always release the "TEST KEY" while changing switch positions. When tuning avoid pressing the test key any more than necessary.

(20) Place antenna transfer switch in trailing antenna position.

(21) Rotate "ANT. IND. TUNING" control "M" to obtain the maximum value of total plate current.

NOTE

Resonance will also be indicated in a secondary sense by the maximum value of antenna current indicated on the "ANT. CURRENT" meter. If no deflection of the plate current meter pointer is indicated or if the maximum plate current is less than 210-220 milliamperes, increase the "ANT. COUPLING SWITCH" "D" and repeat this tuning operation if necessary.

(22) It may be necessary to change the position of the "ANT. CAP. TUNING" control "O" or the length of the antenna and repeat operation (21) before a satisfactory plate loading of 210 to 220 milliamperes is obtained.

(23) The final tuning operation is to move "P. A. TUNING" control "C" to determine if a decrease in plate current, indicated on the total plate current meter, can be produced. If the movement of control "C" which produces the lowest value of plate current exceeds 2 to 3 dial divisions, or if the decrease in plate current exceeds 5 to 10 milliamperes, antenna coupling or antenna tuning adjustments are in error and operation (19) to (23) inclusive should be repeated.

(24) Transmit with the hand key. (See figure 73-18.)

(25) To transmit tone or voice modulated signals, turn the "TONE-CW-VOICE" switch to the applicable position and transmit with the hand key or microphone.

(26) Each time the frequency is changed the transmitter must be retuned accordingly, as outlined in preceding paragraph.

c. TO OPERATE LIAISON TRANSMITTER ON FREQUENCIES BELOW 800 KILOCYCLES.

(1) Reel out all the trailing antenna wire and complete operations included in the preceding operating instructions for the liaison transmitter, except that in operations (6) and (8) position "4" should be substituted for position "2."

(2) If it is impossible to resonate the antenna, set the "ANT. IND. SWITCH" "P" on positions "2," "3," "4," and "5" successively, attempting to resonate the antenna on each position by use of the "ANT. IND. TUNING" control "M."

(3) If operation (2) preceding does not permit resonating the antenna, set the "ANT. IND. TUNING" control "M" and the "ANT. IND. SWITCH" "P" on their maximum positions, set the antenna tuning unit selector switch "E" on positions "2," "3," "4," and "5" successively, and attempt to resonate the antenna by tuning with the "ANT. VARIOMETER" switch "F," on antenna tuning unit, on each position.

(4) Make sure in the preceding operations that sufficient antenna coupling is used and that the plate loading does not exceed 220 milliamperes.

(5) Transmission on "CW" may be effected by use of the hand key, or transmission of tone or voice modulated signals may be accomplished as heretofore noted.

(6) To turn off the transmitter turn the "ON-OFF" switch to "OFF."

NOTE

The maximum specified continuous running time for the transmitter dynamotor is 30 minutes. Always reel in the trailing antenna when communications are completed.

d. OPERATION OF LIAISON TRANSMITTER MONITOR SWITCH.

(1) The liaison monitor switch is located in the radio compass relay shield. This switch is used to enable the operator to quickly tune the transmitter to coincide with the frequency of any desired answering station.

(a) Roughly tune the transmitter to the desired frequency.

(b) Put the monitor switch in the "MONITOR" position.

(2) Listen to desired frequency on liaison receiver and adjust transmitter "M. O. TUNING" control until the transmitter sidetone beats against the desired station signal. The resulting "beat note" will indicate arrival at the proper setting of the transmitter "M. O. TUNING" control.

(3) Put the monitor switch in the "NORMAL" position for regular operation of the liaison transmitter.

e. It is *important* that the radio operator be able to tune to a given frequency quickly. Therefore, the Calibration Chart on the front of the transmitter should be accurate. If a check with the frequency meter shows that the M. O. setting does not coincide with that of the Calibration Chart, check the calibration accuracy observing the following steps:

(1) Set transmitter tuning controls to positions appropriate for CW operation on 11,800 kilocycles.

CAUTION

M. O. control "B" must be set in accordance with the Calibration Chart and locked.

(2) Disconnect transmitter antenna.

(3) Place filament voltage switch in tube compartment in appropriate position.

(4) Place frequency meter in proximity of transmitter. (The frequency meter is located at forward end of main cargo compartment, on left side, lashed to the floor in a horizontal position. The unit is easily removed for use by unbuckling a single strap.)

(5) Place frequency meter in operation and turn on transmitter by throwing "OFF-ON" switch to "ON." (Do not apply transmitter plate voltage.)

(6) Tune transmitter with transmitter antenna disconnected.

(7) Set frequency meter on 11,800 kilocycles in accordance with the operating instructions and calibration chart furnished with the frequency meter.

(8) Open the calibration reset port located on the front panel between the TEST KEY and "TONE-CW-VOICE" switch, insert a screw driver and rotate the calibration screw until the transmitter frequency coincides with that of the frequency meter. Obtain minimum PLATE CURRENT and adjust calibration if necessary until transmitter frequency is set with that of the frequency meter while the PLATE CURRENT meter reading is at minimum value.

(9) Close the calibration reset port. The transmitter is now properly calibrated for any of its tuning units.

(10) Tune transmitter as instructed herein.

f. To obtain dial settings for frequencies falling within the limits of those shown on the Calibration Chart, but not specifically shown thereon, interpolation of dial settings is necessary. (See figure 74.)

(1) Desired operating frequency is 2589 kilocycles.

(2) Dial setting "B" (figure 74-5) for nearest listed higher frequency—2600 kilocycles—is 1289.

(3) Dial setting "B" (figure 74-4) for nearest listed lower frequency—2500 kilocycles—is 1035.

(4) Frequency and dial setting variation—100—254.

(5) Dial variation per kilocycle—2.54.

(6) Interpolation multiplier $= 2589 - 2500 = 89$.

(7) Interpolation product (dial units) $= 2.54 \times 89 = 226$.

(8) Interpolated dial setting $= 1035 + 226 = 1261$.

(9) Set "B" to 2589 by rotating units dial (figure 74-2) until a reading of 12 is obtained on the hundreds scale (figure 11-1) and a reading of 61 is obtained on units scale (figure 74-2).

(f) OPERATION OF FREQUENCY METER SET SCR-211-( ).

1. GENERAL.

NOTE

Inexperienced personnel should not attempt checking frequency of BC-375-( ) transmitter.

a. Secure an antenna, preferably a rigid wire not over two to three feet long, to the antenna terminal on top of the frequency meter cabinet. (Flexible insulated wire may be used.)

b. Plug head set in the phones jack (figure 75-2); turn the power switch (figure 75-3) to "CRYSTAL" position. (Head-set extension cord must be plugged in to complete d-c power circuit to vacuum tubes.) Allow vacuum tube filaments to warm for at least 10 minutes or longer, if necessary as indicated by the drifting of the beat note.

NOTE

Some frequency meters have a power "OFF-ON" switch and a "CRYSTAL OFF-ON" switch.

c. From high or low frequency indices on front and rear covers of calibration book (figure 75-1), determine in which band desired frequency is located and set "FREQ BAND" selector switch (figure 75-9) to correspond.

d. Locate, in the calibration book, the heterodyne oscillator calibration for frequency desired. At bottom of the page will be found the crystal check point (in red) (figure 75-12), together with the heterodyne tuning dial setting (figure 75-13).

e. To set heterodyne tuning control to any desired crystal check point, rotate tuning control until the following readings are observed: (Using 5700 kilocycles as an example for this frequency, the crystal check point is 2070.5.)

(1) The "DIAL HUNDREDS" scale (figure 75-5) should read "20."

(2) The "DIAL UNITS" scale (figure 75-7) should read "70."

(3) The fraction ".5" will be indicated when the fifth outer vernier marking (counterclockwise from the heterodyne control arrow) coincides with the fifth mark past 70 on the rotating inner scale (figure 75-6). (There are 10 vernier markings, each representing one-tenth of a unit.) When the above readings are accomplished, lock the tuning dial.

f. A beat note will probably be heard, as complete absence of beat note can result from only three possible causes: that is, when heterodyne oscillator is exactly on calibration; when it is so far off calibration that beat frequency is above audibility; and when equipment is defective. First two conditions may be determined by rotating "CORRECTOR" dial to where beats become audible. If third condition is the cause, check battery voltages under load. (Filament voltage: 5.4 to 6.0; plate voltage 121.5 to 135.) Adjust heterodyne oscillator frequency by rotation of "CORRECTOR" dial (figure 75.8) until a zero beat is reached.

2. TRANSMITTER ADJUSTMENTS.

a. The method of adjusting transmitter BC-375-( ) to a frequency consists of zero-beating the transmitter frequency with the proper heterodyne oscillator

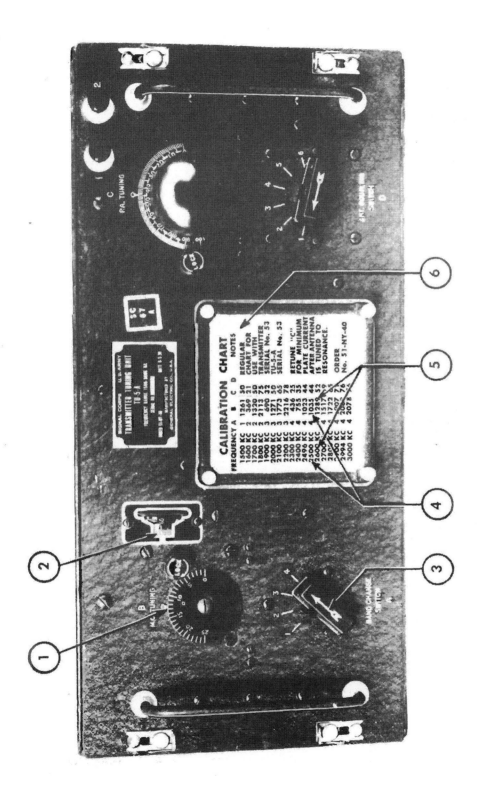

Figure 74—Transmitter Tuning Unit TU-5-A

1. M. O. Tuning Hundreds Scale
2. M. O. Tuning Control "B" Units Scale
3. Band Change Switch "A"
4. Nearest Listed Frequency Below 2589 Kcs
5. Nearest Listed Frequency Above 2589 Kcs
6. Calibration Chart

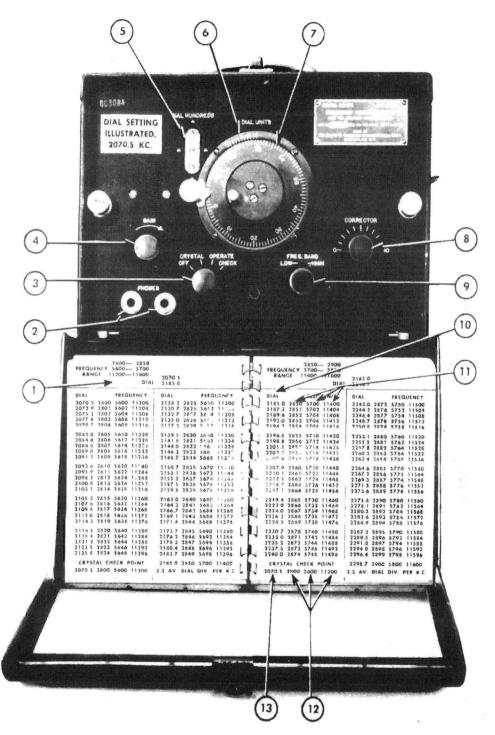

Figure 75—Frequency Meter BC-221-B

1. Calibration Chart
2. Phones Jack
3. Power Switch
4. Gain Control
5. Dial Hundreds Scale
6. Vernier Scale
7. Dial Units Scale
8. Corrector Knob
9. Frequency Band Switch
10. Dial Settings Column
11. Frequency Columns
12. Frequencies Covered By Crystal Check Point
13. Dial Setting for Crystal Check Points

frequency, effecting the comparison by means of a head set plugged into the "PHONES" jack on the front panel of the frequency meter. The "CRYSTAL" switch should be in the "CHECK" position during the process. ("OFF" position on meters having a crystal "OFF-ON" switch.)

b. Specifically, the procedure for adjusting the BC-375-( ) transmitter to a desired frequency is as follows:

(1) Correct the frequency meter heterodyne oscillator to calibration at the crystal check point nearest the desired frequency, as explained under (f)1.e., preceding.

(2) Turn the "CRYSTAL" switch to "CHECK."

(3) Turn the frequency meter tuning control to the dial setting of the desired frequency, as given in the calibration book attached to the meter. Do not disturb the "CORRECTOR" control adjustment obtained in (f)1.f., preceding.

(4) Disconnect the transmitter antenna.

(5) Obtain minimum reading on "TOTAL PLATE" current meter.

(6) Press "TEST KEY" on transmitter and vary "M. O." control "B" until a zero beat is heard in the frequency meter head set. Simultaneously obtain minimum dip on "TOTAL PLATE CURRENT" meter and zero-beat note on frequency meter. Lock M. O. control "B."

(7) Turn off frequency meter and remove head-set cord from plug jack.

(8) Connect transmitter antenna and resonate the antenna quickly to avoid unnecessary station interference.

3. RECEIVER ADJUSTMENTS.

a. The method of adjusting a receiver to a desired frequency consists of tuning the receiver to the proper heterodyne oscillator output frequency, and effecting the comparison by means of a pair of headphones connected to the receiver output circuit.

(1) Correct the heterodyne oscillator to calibration at the crystal check point nearest the desired frequency as explained under "OPERATION."

(2) Turn the "CRYSTAL" switch to "CHECK" and change over to another head set connected to the receiver output jack.

NOTE

If CD-196 or CD-307 extension cord is used in frequency meter, the head set may be disconnected and used in receiver position since the plug operates the power switch, the head set not being required.

(3) Turn the frequency meter tuning control to the dial setting of the desired frequency, as given in the calibration book and lock the dial. Do not disturb the "CORRECTOR" adjustment as made in paragraph 1.

(4) Adjust the receiver for "CW" reception as outlined in preceding operating instructions for the particular receiver to be checked.

(5) With the frequency meter antenna loosely coupled to the receiver antenna lead, vary the receiver tuning control in the vicinity of the desired frequency, listening for the output of the frequency meter. (Signal source may be positively identified by tapping frequency meter antenna with finger and listening for resulting interruption.)

(6) Turn off frequency meter and remove head set from PHONE jack.

(g) OPERATION OF IFF RADIO SET SCR-595.

1. OPERATING COMPONENTS.

a. Turn on the local "ON-OFF" switch on the IFF control box. (See figure 72.)

b. Set the selector switch on the control box to the numbered position designated by tactical orders.

c. If emergency operation is desired, place the "EMERGENCY" switch on the control box to the "ON" position.

d. To turn off the radio set, turn the local "ON-OFF" switch to the "OFF" position.

2. DESTRUCTOR COMPONENTS.

a. The switch controlling the destructor (detonator) unit installed in the IFF chassis is located at the pilot's and copilot's position.

b. To destroy the IFF radio set, if it becomes necessary to do so, raise the hinged cover of the destructor switch and simultaneously press the two switch buttons on the destructor switch.

8. PHOTOGRAPHIC EQUIPMENT.

a. In the aft unpressurized compartment near the auxiliary power plant, provision has been made for the vertical installation and operation of any one of the following cameras: a K-17, K-18, K-19 or K-23, K-21, K-24 or F-24. Also provision has been made for the oblique installation of two K-17 cameras located one on the right, and the other on the left-hand side of the airplane. A stowage bracket located on the right-hand side wall forward of the rear entrance door is provided for the K-20 portable camera, and a motion picture camera, type AN-N-4, is located in each of the five power turrets.

b. Camera openings are provided with skin flush doors which may be operated or removed prior to or during unsupercharged flight. To exclude drafts from the camera compartment, canvas boots are provided which snap fasten to the fuselage and attach with draw strings to the vertical and oblique cameras.

c. The intervalometers, type B-2 or B-3, are mounted above the bombardier's instrument panel and are used in conjunction with the K-17, K-18, K-19, and F-24 cameras and may be preset to automatically operate the camera shutter, by electrical remote control, at specific intervals of time. Remote control of the turret cameras is provided at the individual turret sighting stations.

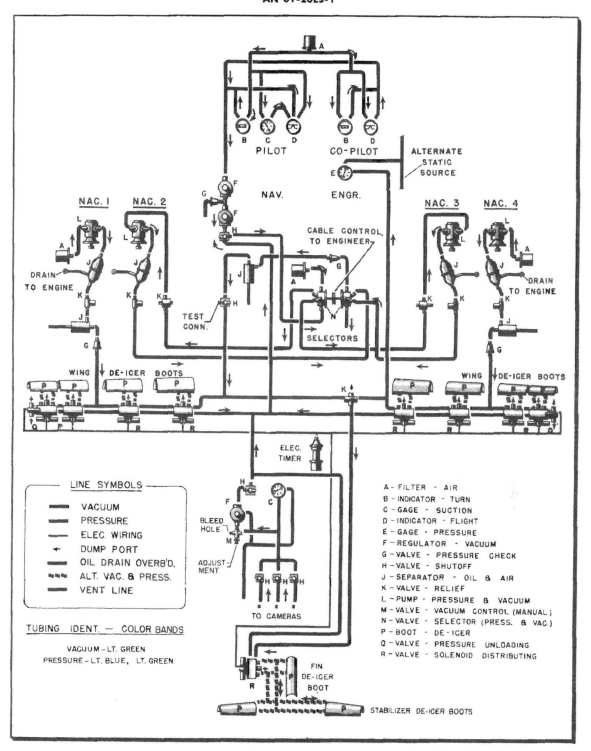

Figure 76—Vacuum and De-Icer Flow Diagram

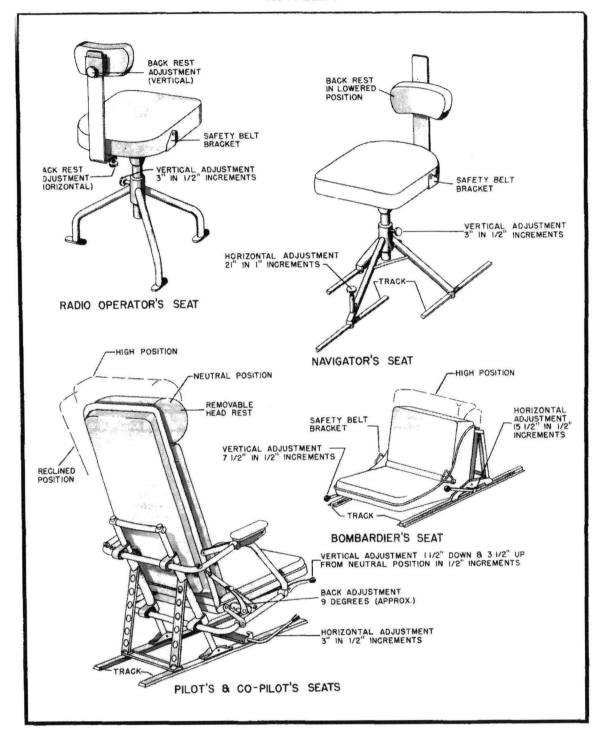

Figure 77—Seat Adjustment Diagram

d. The K-17, in its vertical mount, is used for rapid reconnaissance mapping and is equipped with a 6-, 12-, and 24-inch lense cone; while in its oblique installation it is used for oblique spotting with the 6-inch lens cone. The K-18 camera is used for high-altitude mosaic and spotting. The K-19, with an alternate installation of the K-23, is a night reconnaissance and spotting camera used in conjunction with a photo flash bomb, which may be released from a 100-pound bomb rack by the bombardier. The camera shutter action occurs simultaneously with the explosion of the magnesium bomb. The K-24, with an alternate installation of the K-21, is used for orientation and the F-24 may be used for either day or night reconnaissance and spotting. The K-20 is a portable camera with which photographs may be taken from windows and doors in the airplane, as desired.

9. DE-ICING EQUIPMENT.

a. SURFACE DE-ICER SYSTEM.

(1) A conventional air inflation boot system is used to de-ice the leading edges of wings and empennage. Alternate pulses of vacuum and pressure are supplied from the engine-driven vacuum pumps through solenoid-operated distributing valves. (See figure 76.) The vacuum gage on the pilot's instrument panel has a normal indication of 4 to 6 inches Hg, while the de-icing pressure gage on the engineer's instrument panel has a normal indication of from 7 to 10 pounds per square inch.

(2) A toggle switch on the engineer's switch panel provides control over the de-icing system. Either inboard engine vacuum pump may be selected to provide vacuum for the instruments and de-icer boots, by means of a lever on the engineer's control stand.

(3) In the event of a boot rupture, the entire de-icing system may be shut off by closing the emergency vacuum shut-off valve mounted on the navigator's filing cabinet. This does not affect proper functioning of the vacuum instruments.

(4) When the de-icer system is not in operation, vacuum pump suction prevents the negative air pressure from raising the de-icer boots.

b. PROPELLER ANTI-ICER SYSTEM.—An anti-icing fluid may be pumped to a slinger ring at each propeller from where it is directed to the propeller leading edges. A toggle switch on the engineer's switch panel energizes two electric motor-driven pumps, which direct fluid to the slinger rings at the rate of 2 to 5 gallons per hour. The rate of flow may be controlled by two rheostats located on the lower right-hand side of the engineer's control stand; each rheostat controlling a pump.

10. MISCELLANEOUS EQUIPMENT.

a. SEATS.—(Refer to Seat Adjustment Diagram, figure 77.)

(1) The pilot's and copilot's seats are both provided

Figure 78—Tail Gunner's Seat

with vertical, horizontal, and reclining adjustments; while the bombardier's seat may be adjusted horizontally and vertically. The engineer's seat is not provided with adjustments. The radio operator's and navigator's chairs are the "posture" type and are fixed to the floor; the navigator's chair being on slides and movable parallel with the airplane's center line.

(2) The side gunners' positions are built in the structure and can not be adjusted. The top gunner is provided a stool mounted on a pedestal which may be completely rotated to aid in following a target with his sight. The tail gunner's seat is held up above the gunner's entrance door by springs when not in use, and may be pulled down upon entry to the compartment.

b. BUNKS.—Four bunks are provided in the rear pressurized compartment aft of the armor plate bulkhead, two of which may be used as seats for additional crew members by stowing the top bunks against the side wall of the fuselage.

c. SAFETY BELTS.—Each normal and alternate crew member is provided with a life belt. Troops being transported will be furnished life belts also.

d. LAVATORY EQUIPMENT.—A chemical toilet is provided in the central left portion of the rear pressurized compartment, and a relief tube is located on the navigator's cabinet in the forward compartment.

e. THERMOS JUGS.—Two thermos jugs are supplied; one located on the top of the navigator's cabinet, and the other mounted on the rear compartment auxiliary panel. Paper cup dispensers are provided adjacent to each jug.

APPENDIX I
GLOSSARY OF UNITED STATES - BRITISH NOMENCLATURE

United States	*British*
Angle of attack	True angle of incidence or angle of attack
Angle of incidence or angle of wing setting	Angle of wing setting
Angle of stabilizer setting	Tail-setting angle
Antenna	Aerial
Antifriction bearing	Ball bearing or roller bearing
Battery, storage	Accumulator or storage battery
Beacon, radio range	Radio track beacon
Beam, landing	Approach beam
Bombardier	Bomb aimer
Bureau, weather	Meteorological office
Carburetor	Carburetor
Ceiling	Cloud height
Chord	Chord line
Converter	Motor generator (A.C. to D.C.) or converter
Copilot	Second pilot
Course	Track angle
Distance, take-off	Take-off run
Drift	Drift-angle
Empennage or airplane tail	Tail unit
Engine or power plant	Aero-engine
Field, landing	Landing ground
Flare, signal	Signal star or signal projectile
Flight indicator	Artificial horizon
Gage, fuel, or fuel-level gage	Fuel contents gauge or fuel level indicator
Gasoline, "gas," or fuel	Petrol or fuel
Gear, retractable landing	Retractable undercarriage or retractile under carriage
Generator	Dynamo
Glass, bulletproof, or bullet-resisting glass	Armour glass
Head, air speed	Pressure head
Heading	Course
Interphone	Inter-communication
Inverter	Motor generator (D.C. to A.C.)
Land	Alight
Lean	Weak
Left	Port
Level off	Flatten out
Lights, position	Navigation lights
Longeron	Stringer
Loop, antenna	Loop, aerial
Meter, frequency	Wavemeter
Navigation	Avigation
Nipple	Double-ended union body
Nut, spanner	Ring nut
Operator, radio	Wireless operator
Pad	Accessory mounting face
Panel, inboard	Centre section plane or centre section

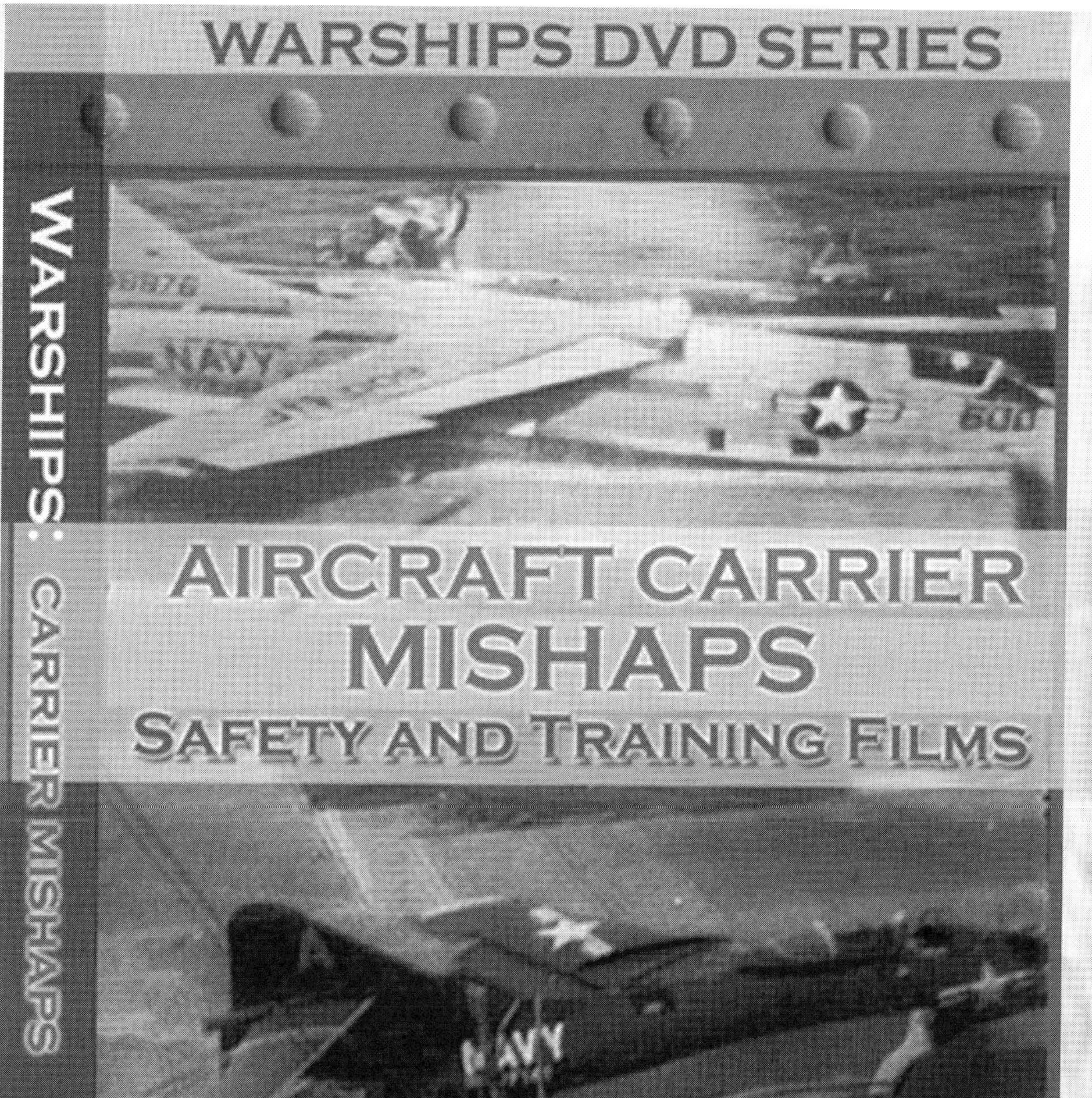
WARSHIPS DVD SERIES
WARSHIPS: CARRIER MISHAPS
AIRCRAFT CARRIER
MISHAPS
SAFETY AND TRAINING FILMS
-PERISCOPEFILM.COM-
DVD
NOW AVAILABLE ON DVD!

Aircraft At War
DVD Series

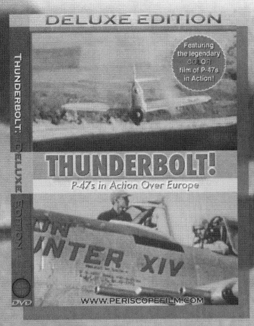

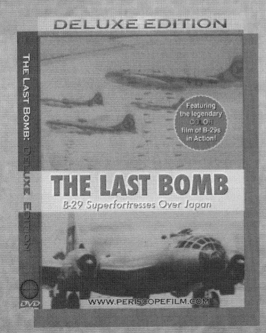

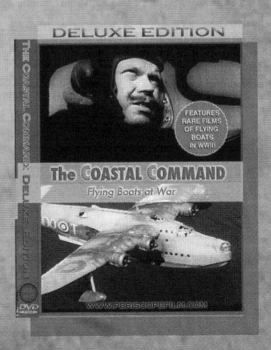

Now Available!

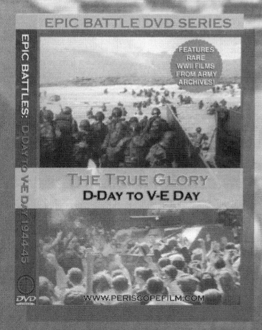

HUGHES FLYING BOAT MANUAL

SPRUCE GOOSE

~~RESTRICTED~~

Originally Published by the War Department
Reprinted by Periscope Film LLC

NOW AVAILABLE!

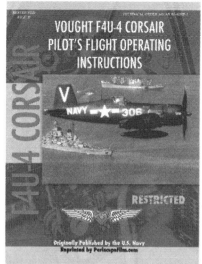
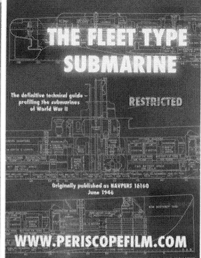

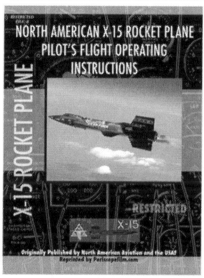
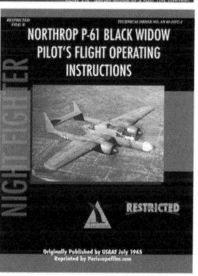
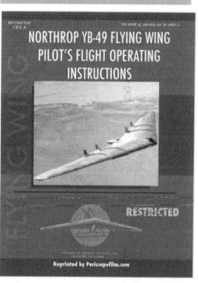

32623157R00058

Made in the USA
Charleston, SC
22 August 2014